Tell Your Story

Learning to tell your story is one of the best ways to improve your life. It gives you clarity about who you are and why you matter, and with that clarity comes confidence. In *Tell Your Story*, Alice Fairfax shows you how. Most people don't realize how interesting they actually are, but with Alice's help, you will.

—**Donald Miller**, *New York Times* best-selling author and CEO of Business Made Simple and StoryBrand

When you see a speaker up on a TED stage, it looks like they are all alone. That's an illusion. Most are backed by a team of deep experts who have helped them hone their message and polish their delivery. Alice Fairfax is one of those experts, and now her wisdom has been assembled in one place for all of us who want our message to reach a broader audience.

—**Dart Lindsley**, head of global process excellence for People Operations at Google and host of *Work for Humans* podcast

When I became a screenwriter, I often gave my scripts to Alice for her unique insight on storytelling. Having known and loved her since our days as audience interactive performers, I greatly value her intuitive observations. Not only is she one of my favorite humans, she simply has an innate talent for finding a story's best path. *Tell Your Story* is filled with gems she has collected over her years of finding and building story in so many settings, and I am delighted the world will get the benefit of her wisdom.

—**Clare Sera**, screenwriter, *Blended* and *Smallfoot*

Your real-life Fairy Godmother strikes again, reminding us of our story-magic that's already within us. *Tell Your Story* is full of possibility that will inspire you on a cellular level, yet is fiercely practical so you feel equipped to take action. This is a must-read if you're ready to captivate the world with your message.

—**Alexandria Agresta**, international speaker, TEDx speaker, and entrepreneur

Alice Fairfax is a writer and storyteller—an artist with an entrepreneurial spirit who knows how to make things happen. She can empower you to focus your message, find your brand, and tell your story. Highest recommendation!

—**Greg Triggs**, author of *The Next Happiest Place on Earth* and *That Which Makes Us Stronger*

A lot of people think they're great storytellers, but the truth is, very few understand the ingredients that make a story zing. Alice is one of those people—she has an inherent grasp on the idea that stories are about *people*, and yet so many leaders forget to include their audience in their narratives. We are in a story culture. The brands and leaders that can put their ideas into compelling yarns are the ones who will thrive. If you want to take advantage of this quickly growing storytelling era, you're going to want to read *Tell Your Story*. And take copious notes.

—**Caitlin Busscher**, content creator and strategist, former Disney ambassador

I've told stories and designed experiences for Disney for almost four decades. I'm a writer by trade, but ask me to explain *how* I tell a story, and you'll get, well, a meandering story. My tale might inspire you, but it will not offer you much help. What Alice Fairfax has done in *Tell Your Story* is make storytelling accessible. It is remarkable, really, how she has not only distilled the practice of storytelling, but she's also explained it in a way that is clear. She offers real-world tools that are usable and a path that is possible. Everyone has a story. Alice will help you tell it.

—**Stacy Barton**, show writer, Disney Live Entertainment

For those lucky readers who are reading *Tell Your Story*, what an incredible gift it is to have such phenomenal insight from one of the industry's best. This is the kind of knowledge people pay top dollar for, so I advise to soak up everything one can and prepare for greatness. I've had firsthand experience working with Alice, and to be able to work with someone who is at a the top of her game, beyond kind, and collaborative is the kind of team anyone wants to be on. I couldn't be more excited and proud to see my friend at this amazing chapter of her life, putting it all out there. Alice is the real deal, and her knowledge is the real deal everyone wants!

—**Michael James Scott**, Broadway actor and singer

Tell Your Stry

TOOLS TO TAKE YOU FROM A TWEET TO A TED TALK

ALICE FAIRFAX

Magic
PRESS
AN IMPRINT OF
MORGAN JAMES
PUBLISHING

NEW YORK

LONDON • NASHVILLE • MELBOURNE • VANCOUVER

Tell Your Story

Tools to Take You from a Tweet to a TED Talk

Published in New York, New York, by Morgan James Publishing in partnership with Magic Press. Morgan James is a trademark of Morgan James, LLC. www.MorganJamesPublishing.com

Proudly distributed by Publishers Group West®

Morgan James BOGO™

A **FREE** ebook edition is available for you or a friend with the purchase of this print book.

CLEARLY SIGN YOUR NAME ABOVE

Instructions to claim your free ebook edition:
1. Visit MorganJamesBOGO.com
2. Sign your name CLEARLY in the space above
3. Complete the form and submit a photo of this entire page
4. You or your friend can download the ebook to your preferred device

ISBN 9781636981444 paperback
ISBN 9781636981451 ebook
Library of Congress Control Number: 2023931952

Cover & Interior Design by:
Christopher Kirk
www.GFSstudio.com

Morgan James is a proud partner of Habitat for Humanity Peninsula and Greater Williamsburg. Partners in building since 2006.

Get involved today! Visit: www.morgan-james-publishing.com/giving-back

Contents

Foreword

I am thrilled to share my thoughts on the exceptional book about storytelling by Alice Fairfax, which is an invaluable resource for anyone looking to become a better storyteller. As a former Disney executive, I know firsthand the power of storytelling to captivate an audience and convey a message that resonates with them on a deep level. This book is an outstanding guide that takes readers through the art and science of storytelling, providing a wealth of practical tools, tactics, and techniques to improve one's ability to craft compelling narratives.

What sets this book apart is how it goes beyond just teaching the craft of storytelling to offering insights into how to use storytelling to improve influence as a leader, be better at marketing, and drive results in any field. Alice does a masterful job of weaving together real-life examples and anecdotes from her experience in the entertainment industry with relevant research and theory to create a highly engaging and informative read.

As someone who has spent his entire career in the business world, and in the Disney theme parks where Alice and I created magic, I found this book to be an invaluable resource that has helped me become a more effective leader and communicator. I highly recommend this book to anyone looking to improve their storytelling skills, whether they are a business leader, marketer, or just someone looking to connect more deeply with others.

—Dan Cockerell, former vice president, Epcot

Introduction

We're in a story culture, and every leader I know feels the pressure to be a part of it—and not only part of it, but great at it.

I know what you're saying: "It's my story—of course I know how to tell it!" And I hear you. Yes, it's your story. But just because you're a great executive director doesn't mean you know how to tell your story. Can you write it as a tweet, a pitch, a TED talk, or a lunch speech for the Rotary Club? Can you send a weekly email campaign infused with the power of story fifty-two times a year? Ah, there's the rub. Your story needs to be clickable. It needs to share the data your board chair wants out there. It needs to lead to a sale or donation. You might even have to get up and tell that story in front of real people, without your hands sweating or your airway clamping shut. Yikes.

You do know your story—but do you know your audience? And what about this particular audience in this particular moment? What if you tell your story beautifully but they don't care how you founded the organization on a dream with your three best friends? What if this group you're talking to wants to know how you made an impact in the last three months? How do you tell the bigger story of what you do with the right examples to connect with the audience in front of you at this very moment?

A story connects ideas and gathers people. When someone sitting across the campfire, writing on the internet, or standing at the front of the room tells a story, what happens? People stop what they're doing. They lean in. Energy pulses through each person, creating a unified energy in the crowd. That energy pulls the thread of our common humanity and draws us into a circle. We're gathered together, fixed on the outcome of this one story.

Can you see the fire circle? People sitting on the ground, the earth warm beneath them as they lean in, listening to the animated storyteller. Each feels a kinship with those next to them as they gasp, laugh, ooh, and ahh together. They're unified. There's power there.

This is because once we're in a story, we don't want to leave. As a listener to a story, we feel two things: belonging and connection. We share a sense of belonging with the community of listeners, those gathered around hearing the story, and we feel mysteriously bonded to the one telling the story too.

The Ancient Tech That Powers the Latest Tech

New technology feels overwhelming. It seems every new platform demands that you, as a leader, not only use it but conquer it. Here's a big secret. It doesn't matter which platform you use. From clay tablets to TikTok, what powers communication now—and always has—is story. There's nothing new under the sun, and the same is true with technology. The most powerful tool the ancients used around the fire circle, at the Pyramids, and on the Great Plains is still available to you now. It hasn't changed. The ancient power of story still fuels the latest technology.

Telling a great story in Pharaoh's temple is no different from telling a great story on Instagram. If you learn the "tech" behind storytelling, which I'll teach you in this book, you can use it on any platform. You can take full advantage of all the places you need to share your story once you know how to tell it. You can become a great storyteller.

Here's why that is powerful. When we listen to a story, we feel connected to the storyteller. As we hear their tale, we believe we come to know them more intimately. Somehow we feel known by them too. We feel seen and heard when a storyteller tells a story, even though we're not the ones speaking. The details of their story may be different, but we want to shout, "Me too!" It's all about the emotions, the feelings, the hopes, and the dreams behind the details. In a very real way, we connect to the story behind the story.

This is the power of story and why using it in everything you do for your business can draw customers, donors, board members, and ideal clients closer to you. Again, we are in a story culture—and that's because story has the power to bond us to each other. Stories connect us for life and turn listeners into loyal followers.

Our Roadmap

In this book, you'll get tools to harness the power of story. With these tools, you can use the power of story to communicate anywhere, anytime, for any audience.

The book is broken into three parts, which mimic the three phases of storytelling.

Phase 1: Discover. Every good story includes a discovery process, where you find the best elements to use in the story. You need to know what your story is really about before you tell it. You know your company's origin stosry, of course, and you might even know your bigger brand story. But you'll connect with more people if you find the deeper story behind either of those things and can craft examples for any situation that allows you to tell that story. That's where we'll start.

Phase 2: Develop. After the discovery phase, stories go into development. This is where the work of writing and crafting a story takes place. You'll discover story process and work on ways to craft your stories. You'll get a bunch more tools. Some of them will work great for you, and some will work perfectly for your managing director or CFO. Some will work in one form (your TED talk) while another will be great in a totally different format (your tweet about your TED talk).

Phase 3: Deliver. Finally, stories are meant to be shared. The last thing we'll do is work on ways to deliver your story. It might be through a speech or a tweet, an email or a proposal. It could mean presenting in person or on video. All those secrets actors know about performing—they'll be yours. In fact, those presentation techniques can help you engage online and in print too.

Additionally, every chapter opens with a story—a picture we'll use to uncover the secrets of how stories work. We'll look at why each of these stories worked, and you'll be given concrete tools you can use to be a better storyteller. You can use the variety of tools placed in your toolkit as you need them to tell your story in a tweet or a speech. You'll even be able to empower your team to do the same.

When we talk about your story, we're talking about the story you need to tell right now, whether it's an annual report that's several hundred pages long or a month's worth of social media posts. We'll also talk about your origin story and mission statement and big brand story, as well as how to drive daily stories into every little tweet. You can apply these story tools to every medium.

I know how hard it is to do this because even though I craft other people's stories for a living, I fall into the same traps you do when having to tell my own. Give you my elevator speech? My bio? A blurb for my books? Uh, well, it all started on a cross-country trip I took with my dad when I was seven...zzzz. Sorry, I put myself to sleep with that story! Just like you, I'm too close to my story. I know it too well. So I use these tools I'm teaching you to dial in on what my audience needs too.

For more than twenty years, I told stories to millions of people—thousands every day. I was an actor and performer doing daily shows on the streets at Walt Disney World. That experience gave me the insight—and the practice—to know how to engage an audience. The storytelling basics, tricks, tools, and tips I employed are all compiled in this book for you.

I'm so glad you don't have to be out in the Florida humidity, trying to gather a crowd at two o'clock on a Thursday afternoon, in order to learn how to connect with an audience in any circumstance. I'll literally save you the sweat. Please feel free to read this in an air-conditioned location. Have a beverage! My fallen arches will be so grateful that their sacrifice provides you with the tools to tell your story.

As you use these tools, you'll start to understand the power of story in even the simplest of circumstances. You'll capture your audience and connect them to your mission—to your heart. You'll communicate your story in ways that connect with the audience in front of you and make an impact on them, which will grow your business and expand your possibilities. You'll be able to use the ancient power of story with today's technology and whatever technology comes next.

It's time to pull back the curtain and discover the secrets the ancients used—the tools and strategies that make a story great.

Part I
Discover

Chapter 1

Make the Connection

Dreams Come True

During the fortieth anniversary year of Walt Disney World, I had a special role as a Traditions assistant. In this job, I facilitated the orientation program for new hires—or, more properly, cast members. The Traditions team learned nomenclature, famous Disney stories, and how to work the sizzle reel and PowerPoint as part of a program so successful, it became the model for employee orientation experiences at other companies. It started, famously, as a three-day program but had whittled down to one day by the time of the fortieth anniversary of the resort.

Still, a full eight-hour-day program is long, and company history and expectations can be didactic. However, the facilitators' storytelling abilities and the immersive program are the hallmark of Disney Traditions. Basically, we tell stories and then we go into the park. When I was a teenager and had a summer job selling Mickey ears, I attended the three-day version of Traditions that included a ride on Space Mountain and a visit to Epcot. In my year as a facilitator, we taught half the day in the conference room, then visited the Magic Kingdom.

In one of my spring sessions, I trained a group of students from Brazil who would work as lifeguards at the pools and waterparks for the summer. These kids were cool. They were tan, young, and exuberant. I felt like their mother in my two-piece black suit and sensible shoes. The first half of the day, I trained them on what was then Disney's Four Keys: Safety, Courtesy, Show, and Efficiency. The kids were polite but not terribly engaged.

After lunch, we headed to the Magic Kingdom, walking through what looked like a very ordinary parking lot behind the shops of Main Street, USA. A van pulled up next to us, and out stepped Bob Iger, then chairman and CEO of Disney, who was hosting several famous business leaders that day. I nodded and greeted him as we do at the first-name company, calling him Bob. My Brazilian teens were unimpressed. They had no idea who he was, even though they'd just watched a video where this man had greeted them on their first day.

We let Bob's group go first as we counted heads. Then I took the lead, my partner took the rear, and we went into the park.

As we turned the corner, there was the castle, gleaming at the far end of Main Street. I explained we would walk together and then stop at the castle, where we would talk some more. Soon, I was surprised to find one of the members of the group, a floppy-haired young man, at my side. He put his arms around my neck and started to cry, soaking the neck of my green blouse.

"This is my dream, my whole life," he said between sobs. We walked the rest of the way to the castle arm in arm, several of his friends linking elbows with us, as we entered his dream come true.

S tories are bigger than the brand. They're bigger than information. They work on two levels—our hearts and our minds. We need the facts in a story, but what makes a super-cool teenager burst into tears is not detailed information. It's something more. Those young lifeguards connected to something bigger than themselves in a unique and specific way when they entered the park.

For your stories to take off, you need to understand the difference between the facts in your story and what your story is really about. That means you need to know the structure behind it—and you can find that structure by using what I call the Story Formula.

The Story Formula

The Story Formula is what makes every story—any story—compelling. It's this: "Universal so we relate. Specific so we care."

To deconstruct the Story Formula, let's look at a story from one of the great communicators, Oprah Winfrey. At the Golden Globes award show in January 2018, Oprah Winfrey received the Cecil B. DeMille award and gave a speech nine minutes long. During that speech and following it, the internet went insane, crying "Oprah for president!" For months afterward, she was chased by the question "Will you ever run?"

The next year, Jeff Bridges received the same award and gave a rambling, dude-esque stroll through memory lane. It was delightfully Jeff Bridges—but no one tweeted "Bridges for President!"

So, what happened? What did Oprah do in that speech?

In my workshops, I play her speech until minute 2:25—because that's all we need to understand how she powerfully used the Story Formula. I recommend you watch the speech, which you can easily find on YouTube by searching "Oprah Winfrey Golden Globes speech." Here are her words from those first few minutes:

> In 1964, I was a little girl, sitting on the linoleum floor of my mother's house in Milwaukee, watching Anne Bancroft present the Oscar for best actor at the 36th Academy Awards. She opened the envelope and said five words that literally made history: "The winner is Sidney Poitier."
>
> Up to the stage came the most elegant man I had ever seen. I remember his tie was white, and of course his skin was black. And I'd never seen a black man being celebrated that. And I have tried many, many, many times to explain what a moment like that means to a little girl, a kid watching from the cheap seats as my mom came through the door, bone-tired from cleaning other people's houses. But all I can do is quote and say that the explanation in Sidney's performance in *Lilies of the Field*: "Amen, amen, amen, amen."
>
> In 1982, Sidney received the Cecil B. DeMille award right here at the Golden Globes, and it is not lost on me that at this moment, there are some little girls watching as I become the first black woman to be given this same award.[1]

What's the difference between Oprah's speech and most award acceptance speeches? Award acceptance speeches, like wedding toasts, are often just a rambling list of thank-yous and details that mean nothing to most people in the audience. When people give us details about an event we weren't part of, we tune out.

Can any of you—any of us—relate to Oprah Winfrey? The answer I always get when I ask this question after showing this video in a workshop is a resounding "Yes! We relate to Oprah!"

"What do you most relate to in Oprah's story?" I ask.

Everyone, without fail, says, "Linoleum floor!"

We remember the linoleum floor. We connect to the linoleum floor.

But that image is not what we actually relate to in her story. I prove this point by next taking a poll. I invite everyone to raise their hand. Then I tell them to drop their hand when something I ask doesn't apply to them. Then I ask:

- Who sat on a linoleum floor as a child?
- Who has watched an old TV?
- Who was once a little girl?
- Who was once a little girl in 1964?
- Who grew up to be Oprah?

I ask them if they know that in one of her houses, I think the one in Hawaii, she had a bathtub cast and carved to perfectly fit her body. Can you relate to that?

We can relate to Oprah, but not because of the specifics in her story. She is actually, factually peerless. No one else has such a unique position in the world. No one else has the platform or reach she does. No one else was a news anchor, then a talk show host, then the star of a Steven Spielberg movie in a role that garnered an Academy Award nomination before becoming a national icon who inspired a generation of people. No one else can say "Been there, done that," except Oprah.

And yet we relate to her story.

That's because her story was universal, by which I mean it contained universal themes. So now I ask:

- Have you ever had a dream?
- Have you ever felt you didn't belong?
- Have you ever seen something that inspired you?
- Have you ever caught a glimpse of who you wanted to be?

Can you relate to those things? Yes, you can. Every day, you experience a desire to be seen and heard, whether in the big arena, like when you see a path to promotion at work and need your boss to see it for you too, or in the daily moments, like when you wonder if anyone other than you ever changes the toilet paper roll. We can relate to Oprah's story, even though it's not our story, because we relate to the theme, or the truth, in it.

Now let's look at why that detail of the linoleum floor lights us up. Imagine our reaction to her Golden Globe speech if it had gone something like this: "You know, I grew up poor, but I dreamed a bigger dream for myself, all because I saw Sydney Poitier get an Oscar. I knew I could make it one day, and now look at me. Here I am, getting the same award he did, and I'm the most powerful woman in the world!"

Do we care? Not so much. We can relate to the theme of dreaming a bigger dream, but this version of the story leaves us out in the cold. We can't care about someone so far removed from us. We can't find a connection point. When did you start to care in her original speech? Say it with me: "Linoleum floor."

We need the specifics so we care. You can see that linoleum floor, can't you? I can even feel it, cool under my feet. In my workshops, we go on to list some of the other things we can see in her story: skin black, tie white, TV, 1964, Milwaukee, sitting on the floor, cleaning other people's houses, little girl. We respond to Oprah's story the way we do because of its universal themes and rich personal details. She shared a motivating over-comer's story while giving us detailed pictures of that story.

I like to think of it the way my dad taught me to trawl for trout. He loves to fish for trout on a lake in north Idaho, where he grew up. I learned from him that rainbow trout are well known for spitting a hook, so there's some work to do getting the fish to stay on your line. In a similar way, there's work to do when reeling your audience in through storytelling. Think of the universal as the reel that casts the idea and the specific as the hook that catches people and keeps them on your line.

Too often when we craft a speech or a pitch or even an email, we tend to fall to one side or the other, either keeping it too universal and out of arm's reach or too in the nitty-gritty details of the specific. When a story remains in the universal, we might be able to relate, but we just don't care. It's above us. It's too lofty. Do you enjoy watching clips of Miss America contestants giving terrible answers to the question round? It's become a cliché: "I want world peace." Those answers don't work because they remain in the universal, floating above us with no anchor in reality. When a story is about a universal theme anyone can relate to but doesn't include any specifics to make us care, our brains hibernate. They think, "This doesn't apply to me."

But a rambling list of minute details doesn't tell the story either. When we go down the rabbit hole of details when telling a story, it's because we're personally reliving it. I listened to a podcast in which a woman told a story about being held at gunpoint and how that moment changed the trajectory of her life. It should have been a compelling story, but she got lost in the details, bogging down the story with what year it was, what room she was in, even what movie she watched the day before—oh, and the movie she watched was a bootleg copy, not even the real one! It was a detail detour leading to a lost opportunity for her to connect with her listeners.

The details of the stories you tell about your business must make a connection to my life and my story. Consequently, your stories must offer more than a laundry list of details.

Universal and Specific

To help you find the universal themes and specific details that work best for a story, let's break up the Story Formula and dive into both parts. Remember, the rule is "Universal so we relate. Specific so we care."

In my full-day workshops, we take two big flip-chart pages and stick them next to each other on the wall. At the top of one, I write "Universal." On the other, "Specific." Then we call out words for each list, starting with the universal. The goal of this exercise is to help you see that you can drive your universal themes higher and higher, broader and broader. Then on the specific page, you can go deeper and deeper while adding more detail.

Invariably, when we start with universal, the participants start small. A nonprofit food pantry list might look like this:

Universal
Hunger
Lost wages
No food

"Go higher," I'll say.

"What do you mean?" they ask. "Hunger is universal."

"Is it, though?" I reply. "It's eleven thirty and we have lunch at noon, and I'm starving. But am I really starving? Am I really even hungry? Can I *really* relate to hunger?"

I can't. I have no idea what it means to experience the kind of hunger we're talking about. How can I, who had an egg sandwich and an Americano at eight thirty this morning and am now "starving" for lunch, really relate to the needs of those served by the food pantry?

Now they start getting into it and yell words faster than I can write:

Universal
Fear
Uncertainty
Need

Want
Desire
Power
Loss

"Yes! That's it," I say. "I can relate to all of those things."

Then we move those original three words they said to the "Specific" list and start adding more. "Get lower now!" I tell them. "Start with hunger and tap into your five senses—what do you see, smell, taste, touch, hear?" The list of specifics starts to look like this:

Specific
Hunger
Lost wages
No food
Growling stomach
Bad taste on my tongue
Dirty hands
Walking to a job
Taking the bus
Kids with dirty T-shirts
Dollar menu
School lunch on a tray
Wrapping half the sandwich from the school lunch in a napkin and shoving it into a backpack to take home for my baby brother

Now look at both lists. We have a story that's universal so we relate and specific so we care. It's a story about the fear and uncertainty in a child who ate his last meal at eleven thirty in the morning at school but carries half the sandwich in his backpack until four thirty, when he can share it with his baby brother. I feel the fear in that story because I know fear in my own life. And I care about it because I can see the backpack and smushed PB&J sandwich.

When listeners hear that a food pantry serves students who go hungry after school, that sounds important but means nothing to them. They can't hear it, taste it, see it, smell it, or touch it. When they hear the same information shared as a story about an eight-year-old boy, though—one your organization serves who has his last meal for the day at eleven thirty, then wraps half of his peanut butter and jelly sandwich in a paper napkin and puts it at the bottom of his backpack, where it gets crushed by his notebooks, so his four-year-old brother gets to have dinner that day—this alerts the listeners to their own survive-and-thrive instincts. Those instincts say, "This is a dangerous situation. This has immediate impact on my ability to survive and thrive in this society. If one of my tribe is going through this, that means we, as a group, are not surviving and thriving. This could be happening in the school my children attend. This could, heaven forbid, happen to me and my family."

Using this technique, you can find stories in your organization. From the food pantry list, you can find other stories. Do you also see the story of a person riding multiple buses to get to a part-time job that pays nine dollars an hour? Did you see the mom purchasing dinner for a family of five from the dollar menu? We did. These events happened. They're not fiction; they're examples. They're true stories your executive director might already have told to donors, to your board, or at fund-raising dinners. I use this listing exercise for every story I tell, whether it's for a book, web copy, a press release, or an Instagram post. I recommend using the side-by-side lists so you can really see the difference.

We're looking for a compelling way to share these kinds of stories so the hearer's brain engages on the deepest level. We're looking for a theme in the story that's universal—hopefully something I, the listener, am going through right now, which makes it important to me. And we're snapping into that theme because of the linoleum floor, the gleaming castle, or the backpack. These give us a specific picture, which makes us pay attention.

Just like Oprah, you can connect with your audience through shared universal themes and rich personal detail. You find your stories by driving those universal themes to their highest, most relatable level and then diving down into the most vibrant details of situations. Your audience will connect through the universal themes, and they'll remember the specifics.

Engage with Action

Once you discover the universal and define your specifics, it's time for action. Make the story exciting! Now we get to play and dress them up. Action becomes the third giant paper we stick on the wall in my seminars.

By action, I simply mean verbs. We aren't plotting the action in our stories just yet. First we need verbs in our sentences. How many stories have you heard that started "I want to tell you about…" Oh boy, you know you're in for a long ride then. We don't want to talk *about* an event, we want the audience *in* the event.

The word *about* is an indicator for me to check out. I've heard millions of pitches that start something like this: "I want to tell you about our organization and one of our students who really benefitted from your donation. This student had been receiving support from their school when their father, who had been using drugs..." This is a passive state. The action is happening to the character, rather than the character taking action. "The student had been receiving." In other words, they were just sitting there when one day, donations dropped out of the sky.

We need to get our sentences into an active state. An easy way to tell if you're writing or speaking passively is to count how many verbs there are in a row. Look at "The student had been receiving." That's three verbs: *had, been,* and *receiving.* In the same way, too many "About" sections on company websites start something like this: "We had been talking about starting this business when we realized that we both had a passion for marketing." There are six verbs in that sentence. Imagine each one as a wave of warm air. The reader is lulled to sleep by the time they get to the point of the story. Try these instead: "We talked." "We realized." "We launched." "We needed."

In your story, things didn't happen to you or at you. You were in it. Bring us into the story, too, with action verbs. We need action verbs to move the story along.

When I worked with a company that offered summer camps at a local theater, here were some of the action verbs we tried in this list exercise:

Action
Play
Teach
Stand
Run
Jump
Memorize
Sing
Project
Laugh
Listen
Act
Read
Stretch
Dress
Bow
Applaud

Now bring the three lists together. The three lists for this theater summer camp might include:

Universal	Specific	Action
Confidence	Pink costume	Memorize
Being heard	Bare stage	Play
Fear	Red velvet audience chair	Project your voice
Nerves	Hands	Clap
Together	Blackout	Sing
Alone	Stage lights up	Gasp
Being seen	Arms out	Bow
Accomplishment	Summer camp	Laugh

Start at the universal and pick one. Match it with a specific, and then pick an action verb. Do you see a story start to come together? Do you see the threads of it? It might sound like this: "Our summer camps start on a bare stage. Kids enter that first day nervous and excited. Each day they build confidence while they build the set, rehearse the lines, and glue sequins on pink costumes. Until the last day, when their families take a seat in the red velvet chairs of the theater, the lights come up, and we hear the whole audience gasp. They did it. Take a bow." That's a possible story version of "Our summer camps provide kids the opportunity to build confidence and learn collaboration while experiencing the satisfaction of achieving a common goal." Which is stickier? Which version will you remember? Which one can your audience picture? These are the questions you need to consider when you share what you do, wherever you share it.

I often lead a yearly workshop for a variety of nonprofits at one time. We might have a food pantry, a farm collective, an opera company, a special-needs service organization, a counseling ministry, and a dance troupe all in the same room. At a recent session, the opera company asked the group to do this exercise with them. The first time we did it, the clear audience was opera patrons—those who attend the performances. We found aspirational universal themes of beauty, meaning, and escape, and we named specifics like sequins, ties, perfume, and programs. The actions included breathing, holding a note, and getting goosebumps.

This was just one aspect of the company, though. We did the same exercise for their school program. Three sheets of paper on the wall again, and we found universal themes of esteem, respect, belonging, and recognition. We found the specifics of a seven-year-old boy, a six-year-old girl, tiny desks, sitting cross-legged in a circle, hands on bellies, children's voices, Brahms's "Lullaby," and "This Old Man." And we found the actions of introducing, conducting, singing, laughing, hearing, breathing, learning, and discovering. With the list of action verbs next to the lists of universal and specific, they had several stories to follow.

Action is what makes a story move. It's the catalyst and the driver for each story. If the only tool you ever use to tell your story is this tool of making three lists—universal, specific, and action—you'll offer compelling stories that get your audience asking, "And then what?"

Takeaways:

✓ Remember the Story Formula: "Universal so we can relate. Specific so we care."
✓ Find your universal themes by driving higher and higher.
✓ Find the specific details by digging deeper and deeper. Remember the linoleum floor.
✓ Find action by naming verbs.
✓ Build stories through the use of three lists: Universal, Specific, Action.

Chapter 2

Flip the Script

Feliz Navidad, Mickey

I was a storyteller in Mexico. Not the real Mexico—the mini fake one at Epcot. As an actor at Walt Disney World, I was part of a troupe that got shipped to different countries from Thanksgiving through New Year's Eve. I told the story of the holidays in Germany, Italy, the United Kingdom, and—one random year—Mexico.

For the show, I played an adventurer just back from Mexico who was there to interview one of the Mexican students in the pavilion. The student and I would then share the tradition of Las Posadas. Eight times daily, I gathered children on a stage built onto the street outside the pavilion and told them a story. Other guests wandered by with margaritas while I handed out scarves, hats, and props for the audience to dress up as the characters from the Nativity story.

Then we would enact Las Posadas, a parade traditional in Mexican neighborhoods where families go from house to house, knocking on doors and asking for hospitality. At each door, they are turned away—until they reach the last house, where there's "room at the inn" and a party ensues. Our show ended with all the children saying "Feliz Navidad!" to the gathered crowd.

Adorable. Except for the 5:15 show.

The 5:15 show followed the five o'clock tree lighting in the center of the park. Mickey, Minnie, Goofy, Donald, and all the other Disney characters sang songs, then lit the tree. Then they boarded a red double-decker bus and drove away to the cheering of the audience, heading right through—you guessed it—Mexico.

The bus full of characters arrived in Mexico at about 5:17, right when all the children and families were waiting to be part of our show. From 5:15 until 5:20, instead of starting the script, I had to make sure no one got run over by Mickey Mouse.

Not only was this a very un-magical experience, but it was also a safety hazard. I emailed my boss, the director of the show, to say that while we hadn't lost anyone yet, it just wasn't much fun. I asked if we could flip the script and bring all the kids on stage first. We could teach them to say "Feliz Navidad," which is "Merry Christmas" in Spanish. Then, after the bus went by, I could hand out props and give everyone a character for Las Posadas.

This was a big ask. You don't just change the direction of a show at Walt Disney World. Scripts go through multiple layers—or, as I always say, two Imagineers and a show director—for approval. I should also mention this was not the usual Mexico holiday show. Every year prior, the Three Kings had come out in flowing, beautiful robes to tell their stories. It was very presentational, using formal costumes, formal voices, and lots of fake beards. But that show needed a refresh, and because I had expertise in audience interaction, I was invited to put this new show up.

The Three Kings costumes were pretty fabulous—and pretty expensive—so I knew our version of the show likely wouldn't last. My hope was that if I could work this script well enough, it would give the leadership something more engaging to use with the Three Kings. I would also be seen as a valuable creative asset, and then I could go back to Germany, where I belonged.

My director responded with the instruction to try my idea three times. She would come to see it the third time, to approve or not.

The first night, my student co-star and I gathered the kids on stage and got their family members out of the way. No one got run over, but it wasn't great.

The next day, I emailed the character leads from Mickey's show and told them we'd be waving at them that night, calling out "Feliz Navidad" as they rode by. We tried it that night, and it went better. The characters drove by, waving back to us. It was certainly more efficient and allowed the bus to move right along.

Better, but still not magical.

When one of the character leads replied to my email that night, I may have mentioned my director was coming to the show the next day. Showtime came and, as expected, the director stood in the crowd on the opposite side of the street. The bus was heading our way, and we saw every character on the bus dancing to the music. Only this time, when they reached Mexico, they stopped. There Mickey stood, on top of the double-decker bus, in his holiday outfit of a plaid vest and festive hat.

Like magic, a spotlight shone down from the pavilion's pyramid, illuminating Mickey's face. He looked down at us and in classic Mickey style put his hand to his ear and hit a pose. The kids went nuts. They jumped up and down as they screamed, "Feliz Navidad, Mickey!" He smacked his hands to his heart, and the rest of the characters erupted, waving and blowing kisses to the kids.

The parents were teary. I was teary. I looked over at the director, who was also teary. We had saved Christmas.

That year, the 5:15 show became one of the more popular times to see the Mexico show. We went from five kids to thirty each night. These were the days before mommy bloggers and Instagram, but somehow word got around that if you couldn't get a good spot at the tree lighting, head over to Mexico—not only would you get to see the characters, but your kids would be on stage, get to interact with the characters, and still be in a cute show.

The "Feliz Navidad, Mickey" script didn't work any other time of day. It only worked at that particular moment, for that particular set of circumstances. We flipped the script to meet the moment.

Most leaders know the importance of telling stories about the amazing things their companies do. You likely know stories help move the needle—in awareness, engagement, donations, and clientele. But most small business leaders also manage payroll, lead teams, plan fundraisers—oh, and don't forget to drop by Staples to pick up more copy paper.

When you're the marketing director for a nonprofit or the communications manager at a startup, you might hear board members or your CEO say things like, "Why doesn't anyone know the amazing things we're doing?" Or my favorite: "You need to make a video that goes viral!"

It's harder than it sounds, though, isn't it?

When I was an actor at Disney World, my job was to tell stories—and not just to tell them, but to bring unsuspecting audience members out of their seats and onto the makeshift stage to become part of them. I worked with many people who were naturals at asking audience members to interact. I was not one of them. I was theater trained and terrified of giving audience members the power to interact with the show—with *my* show. How do you pick someone who won't mess it up? What do you do when the story veers in a different direction? How do you get the audience on your side? How do you get them to do the things you ask them to do?

There wasn't a manual on how to do it, so I watched people who were so good at it, they couldn't have explained it if they tried. That's how I learned to tell stories and engage an audience—and that's where I learned about the difference between the key elements in a story and the more modular ones that can shift around, depending on the need of the moment.

Another place I learned to connect stories to a particular moment was at a large church in Orlando led by Dr. Joel Hunter, a gifted speaker who in 2008 was invited by then Senator Barack Obama to give the closing prayer at the Democratic National Convention. At the church he led, members would sometimes come on stage to address those in the room, which could number up to three thousand people, plus several thousand more who tuned in via live-stream from their homes and coffee shops. Those poor people on stage fell apart. Their voices pitched up or they ran out of breath. They tried to create interesting stories the way Dr. Hunter did because they wanted to engage the crowd the way he did, even if their message only announced new parking procedures. But Dr. Hunter was a born speaker and storyteller. This was everyone's problem—they were trying to be their best *him*, not their best *them*.

To help, I created a training session for the church's department leaders. We covered how to speak, how to breathe, and how to manage what happens to your body when you get up in front of more than three thousand people. We worked on mining content to find the best story, then how to craft the story and tell the story. We practiced ways of telling the story to the five o'clock crowd, which carried a different energy than the ten o'clock group.

Maybe you've got questions about how to win a crowd, how to find the right story, and how to adjust a story when telling it to a couple donors versus a group of two hundred. Oh, and don't forget the need to be fresh and true in both situations. Leaders like you are often asked to give speeches because they're good at their job as the CEO, entrepreneur, or nonprofit founder—but being great at what you do doesn't mean you know how to give a speech about it! Someone who's good in a room while leading a team of five might not be great at giving a keynote address to five thousand. And then there's the question of how to get everyone on the team to tell the same brand story without becoming bizarre brand robots.

I promise you can learn to tell your story in compelling ways that meet the need of each moment. You, too, can flip the script of a story to meet your audience where they are. The main thing to know is that some story elements must always be shared, while other pieces are modular and can shift around. You've already discovered that the Story Formula must always be present in every story. Let's dig a little deeper.

Give Them Brain Food

The story you're telling right now is likely focused on the facts. Facts are important, but listing facts—on your website, on your product label, in every speech you give—isn't telling your story. You have a message that, when delivered as a story and adapted for the moment, will connect. It will grow your audience and drive more business.

To flip the script and meet the moment, you need to start by knowing that story is how we process information. We've known this for years—millennia, really. Go back to the fire circle and our ancestors, who gathered around to tell and listen to stories. They shared stories about their days and their experiences. They revisited stories, like the time that mammoth kill was so awesome. The fire circle helped them chronicle what worked and what didn't. Stories show us the strategies of individuals who triumphed in similar circumstances. It's how history teaches us to learn from our mistakes.

Stories still help our brains figure out ways to overcome whatever difficulties we're facing today. It's like practicing a Rubik's cube. If we can train our brain to sort through information and find a way to make something work in a game, then we can do it in real life. More than inspirational, stories show us that we can overcome. We can figure things out. Our ancestors overcame a plague, a siege, or an obstacle similar to one we're now encountering. We will too. Stories train our brains to know we can overcome, and they even show us how to overcome.

The philosopher Aristotle talked about this in his work *Poetics*. I first encountered this slim book when it was assigned in my freshman high school theater class. I kept it for years, my copy eventually becoming tattered and yellowed. Aristotle spoke to me from thousands of years ago about the importance of acted-out stories: "It is for this reason that men enjoy looking at images, because what happens is that, as they contemplate them, they apply understanding and reasoning to each element."[2]

It's no different now. We enjoy looking at images, memes, videos, and reels that help us contemplate our stories too. Instagram, YouTube, Netflix, and Facebook are like the theater of the ancient Greeks. This is where we share our stories now, making our voices heard. We share the power of our overcoming, and we get power from other people's victories.

Mike McHargue—aka Science Mike, a wise fellow with a podcast called *Ask Science Mike*, who shares insights like a modern Aristotle—confirms our brains are designed to survive and thrive. He says that in an effort to conserve brain calories for survival, they sort through unless information but hold on to stories.[3] Stories provide the protein our brains need to keep going.

Similarly, renowned neuroscientist David Eagleman reports, "The unconscious brain is ruthlessly efficient. It is looking for the easiest path [to a solution]."[4] When you're trying to engage your audience, a story is the easiest path for the unconscious brain to follow.

Donald Miller, author of *Building a StoryBrand*, says story organizes information. That means we don't have to expend energy organizing it for ourselves. Story feeds our need for survival by giving us a straight line from here to there—a character has a problem, and the story shows us how to solve it. Stories tell our brain, "This is important. Listen to this, and you'll learn how to survive a zombie apocalypse, get back to Kansas, and defeat the Empire with only a few rebel spies." Those are specific stories, but think about the universal "story behind the story" for each one, as we've been discussing. They teach us how to survive a worldwide trauma or plague, how to get back home or to your center, and how to overcome an overwhelming evil power. Sounds like useful information.

Story is brain food. We want to know how someone else did it—how they survived and thrived. We want to know: "How do I make it too? How do I get from here to there?" We want the people who have gone before us to tell us—but if they tell us in a PowerPoint with graphs and charts, we usually tune out. We believe them, but our brains push the plate aside to save calories. Where's the beef? It's in the story.

Stories of Survival

In my workshops, I start by telling the "Feliz Navidad, Mickey" story. Then I put my résumé on the screen. Here it is:

Alice Fairfax

A sought-after creative leader
with expertise in training, speaking, and writing.

Experience

DTGO/MQDC, October 2022–Present
Sr VP Ideation & Experience Design

- Design & deliver narrative design for theme destinations
- Lead trainings for key stakeholders from branding through the customer journey
- Connect the story through every aspect, from high concept to retail design to guest-facing team.

Dr. Phillips Center for the Performing Arts, September 2014–August 2021
PR Leader, Creative Team Manager, Copywriter

- Manage all aspects of PR plans and publicity tours for shows, pitching story ideas to media, coordinating schedules, setting up interviews, serving as an ambassador in print and on camera

Walt Disney World, February 1996–August 2014
Disney Institute, Content Developer, Special Project, March 2014–August 2014

- Develop materials that are creative, engaging, relevant, and appropriate to the course topic and delivery method
- Establish partnerships with facilitators, graphic designers, app developers, stakeholders, and clients

Disney Event Group, Script Writer & Site Visit Facilitator, November 2012–March 2020

- Write executive speeches, proposals and scripts

- Facilitate presentation with Sales Managers for potential clients and meeting planners
- Partner with Entertainment, Floral, Creative Directors, Producers, Costuming, Actors, and Sales to prepare client discovery information and present creative ideas for customized events

The American Idol Experience, Casting Director, January 2011–August 2014

- Interact with up to 50 guests daily, host individual auditions, cast guest singers, and send to producer level
- Coach guests on performance

Entertainer and Coach, February 1996–December 2010

- Train Entertainment Cast Members and manage performance quality
- Entertain Walt Disney World guests daily through storytelling, interaction, improvisation, and musical theater performances portraying a variety of characters, including one iconic Disney character (be sure to ask which one!)

Did you read it? Were you moved by it? Didn't you love the part where I talked about developing relationships with key stakeholders and app developers? Riveting. I can almost guarantee you didn't read it. Maybe you didn't even bother to skim it. The reason is, my résumé won't help you survive.

Here's the funny thing. My résumé and the "Feliz Navidad, Mickey" story give you the exact same data. You learn from both that I'm a storyteller with the credentials to lead you through this material. Looking at the résumé, you might pick up a few data points that impress you enough to be willing to listen to me. But more likely you won't look at it—and even if you do, nothing will stick. The data won't mean anything to you.

After I show my résumé to workshop participants, I ask them to go back to the "Feliz Navidad, Mickey" story and tell me its data points. They usually say:

- "You know how to think on your feet."
- "You know the importance of process."
- "You were a storyteller at a place famous the world over for storytelling."
- "You worked with Mickey Mouse."
- "You know how to get in front of people and speak."
- "You know how to memorize a fifteen-minute show."
- "You understand the basics of storytelling and how to engage an audience."

When I ask how the story helped them, they say it showed that I can help them tell their stories too. Then I ask what the story was about. Was it a cute story used to get them engaged, like an icebreaker? Was it a survival story? They're usually fifty-fifty between the two.

Let's think about this. You may not have ever told a story at a theme park, but there are other people on the planet who have—people who are Disney-actors-turned-workshop-leaders like me. You may not have ever told a story in Epcot to children during the holidays, but there are others who did and do, and they can certainly relate to my story. But why is this story not just for a group of people who once were storytellers at Epcot? Because it's universal so you can relate and specific so you care.

If our brains process stories to survive and thrive, then how does this story of the holidays at Epcot speaks into the universal theme of survival? Let's look at the universal themes in it: a job that isn't working, people counting on you to make something work, concern for the safety of the people in your charge.

I could have told the "Feliz Navidad, Mickey" story in a purely thematic way. It would have sounded something like this: "I was a storyteller at a major theme park in Orlando, and I was having trouble in one of the shows. So I talked to my boss and changed the flow of the story, and it worked!" That's nice. Who cares? No one. That summary bounces right off. You can feel your brain gaining weight from holding those calories. It's the specifics of the double-decker bus and the little kids and the holiday sweaters and the Mickey Mouse glove and the spotlight on Mickey that connect you to the universal themes in that story.

When you break down the story, you see it's a story about a woman who needs to make her job work but has hit an obstacle to her success. She tries and she tries, until one day she figures it out. She turns a poorly performing show into a triumphant moment. Her boss sees it, and her job is safe. That's a survival story.

Then I tell them the rest of the story. I was back in Orlando after a disastrous move, separated and on the brink of divorce. I was living at my parents' home with my seven-year-old son. I had worked at Walt Disney World before, but I wasn't guaranteed a contract in the new year. As soon as New Year's Day came, my holiday storytelling gig would finish, and I might be out of a job. Seen through this lens, I had to figure out the 5:15 show. I couldn't let it slide as a sparsely attended, boring show no one knew or cared about. I had to make it work. My future was at stake.

All the data my résumé tells you—that I'm a writer, I'm a speaker, I collaborate with teams, and I drive solutions—shows up in the "Feliz Navidad, Mickey" story too. But the story carries an undercurrent of high-stakes need in a fun setting. It's memorable. And what really connects is not the Holiday Mickey part of the story. It's the story of survival.

I usually ask my workshop participants, "How many of you can relate to being the Mexico storyteller at Epcot?" No hands go up. Then I ask, "How many of you can relate to being in a job where you had to make it work or you might not move forward—or worse, might lose your job?" Most hands go up. My story is about surviving and thriving. Your story is about surviving and thriving too.

From Survive to Thrive

Survival stories are all well and good when your organization feeds hungry children. But what about when you work at an art museum, a ballet, or an opera? How do you compete with an organization like charity: water or the Gates Foundation? What if you're a marketing consultant or a food blogger?

A story can teach us ways to thrive. *You've Got Mail* showed us how to find our one true love. *The Devil Wears Prada* gave us a path to overcome the mean boss and become our own person. And because of Elizabeth Gilbert, we all know how to eat, pray, and love our way back to a vibrant life after a divorce.

A thrive-focused organization and a survive-focused non-profit don't usually compete for dollars—except in the case of the Victory Cup Initiative, a yearly competition in Orlando where ten nonprofits attend a breakfast with hundreds of companies and their corporate responsibility directors. Each nonprofit sends a person, and that person gets two minutes and thirty seconds to tell the story of their nonprofit to this powerful group. The organizations run the gamut, from homeless shelters to pet rescues to children's cancer research charities to dance troupes.

It's set up as a competition because that's sexy. It's what brings people to the breakfast. But in my job of preparing the storytellers, during the day of training I spend with them, I repeat over and over that even though it's a competition, it's not a competition. It's an opportunity.

One year, the children's theater company found itself facing off against a children's cancer research charity founded by a mother whose son overcame cancer and who was convinced by her experience that the research to fight childhood cancer was inadequate. Oh, and she's Scottish, so she has a lovely accent.

Folks, nobody wins against that.

The board chair of the children's theater, an engaging and entertaining man with a great story to tell, kept defeating himself by focusing on the competition. "There's no way we're going to win," he said during the workshop to everyone, including the Scottish mom.

I was straight-up honest. "You're right," I said. "I'm in the arts, and we don't beat kids. We don't beat cancer. We don't beat hunger. We rarely ever go up for the same dollars, because we won't win."

Then I gave him two reasons to stay and tell his story and the story of his organization. First, winning is not the point of telling your story. Your story may provide a solution to someone else's problem that day. Several hundred people representing several thousand dollars of corporate funding would be at this event. It's always a win to get a platform to share your story. While there are winners—$10,000 for third place; $15,000 for second place; $20,000 for first place—the competition is just advertising for the event. It's a fun game to get people in the door. Then, once they're inside, they get to hear ten stories. Victory Cup storytellers have gone on to gain board members, volunteers, and individual gifts. They've been handed anonymous donations and been invited to apply for grants. They've learned to tell their stories so well, they've gained national media coverage.

The second reason to tell your story is that people need to thrive, not just survive. Once someone gets out of the survival stage, they'll cast their gaze upward. They want to move past surviving into thriving. A mom wants her child to play a musical instrument, participate in sports, or star in a play. The reason to survive is to get a chance to thrive, just as this mother did once her son survived childhood cancer.

I know this to be true because it was my path with my child too. In the mid 1990s, when my son, Henry, was diagnosed with autism, very few resources were available. We survived his behaviors, such as refusing to sleep for more than an hour at a time or smearing his feces into the CD-ROM drive of the computer every single day. I put him on a special diet. I bought a $50 bottle of vitamins over the internet when Amazon was still just a bookstore. We lived in a tiny apartment with two bedrooms and one bathroom. I quit my job and worked part-time. We went to physical therapy, occupational therapy, and speech therapy. We moved closer to the only school that served kids with autism.

When Henry's behaviors were under control, he started doing his own talk show on YouTube. He joined a theater group and hosted a dance recital at an arts center. He moved past surviving. He began thriving. For my part, sacrifice and survival had been my way for so long that I didn't know how to thrive. It took many months, probably years, for me to give up my survival habits. And it took organizations like the Orlando Museum of Art, where I could go and look at beauty, just because, and the Orlando Repertory Theatre, where we could attend sensory-friendly performances for children like Henry, to get me there. It took theater and music—things meant for my enjoyment and pleasure.

I relied on some organizations to provide me with a foundation for the basics, and they helped me survive. But the reason for me to survive was so that one day, we could do something beautiful with Henry's gifts. Thriving gives us a reason to survive. Don't count your story out.

Pyramid Scheme

The best tool to use to know where your organization sits when it comes to surviving or thriving is Maslow's hierarchy of needs. You're probably already familiar with this. A quick internet search will provide you with many illustrations of the original hierarchy, which is usually pictured as a pyramid. The base of the pyramid consists of our basic survival needs: food, water, shelter. Once those basic needs are met, we move to the next level up, which is security: job, health, property. As we meet the needs on this platform, we keep ascending, reaching for love and belonging, then esteem, and eventually the final tier, which is self-actualization. The point of the hierarchy is to say that if you're hungry, you aren't going to attend a three-day retreat to center yourself and cast a vision for your dreams. But once you've moved up the pyramid, getting a vision for your life becomes important.

The *Harvard Business Review* expanded on Maslow's hierarchy with its "Elements of Value" pyramid.[5] It provides a particular focus on how to communicate business to business and can be helpful if your work is in marketing. The base of this pyramid is not survival but the functional needs of your customers. Does your brand help customers make money, reduce risk, or save time? These are labeled functional needs. Then it drives up through emotional needs, such as reducing anxiety, providing access, and fun, until it reaches the final two tiers, which relate to life change and social impact.

The thing about both pyramids is that when we're on the lower levels, we always need to look up toward something else. When I was out of work and raising a small child with autism, I wasn't booking a Byron Katie retreat. I was, however, dreaming of being something more than I was at that moment. The dream of going to a retreat with the white-haired Katie, sipping tea and discovering my turnarounds, was very motivating for me while scrubbing out the computer keys with a brush.

We're all looking up the ladder to see what comes next. We want to see a light at the end of the darkness we're experiencing at the moment. The best stories—the ones that keep *CBS Sunday Morning* going—are the overcoming stories. They're the ones where someone had nothing, saw something above themselves, and reached for it.

To find where your business sits on the pyramid, consider not only what your organization offers but what your audience needs. I often use the ballet as an example for this because it's one of the hardest organizations to fundraise for. Why? Because the dancers make it look effortless. What goes into that dance, however, is hours of rehearsal. Dancers are athletes, so they have personal trainers, massage therapists, physical therapists, and a multitude of toe shoes. Ballet companies need money to make things look easy.

Now think about the audience the ballet company is trying to reach. What do they need? Ballet makes us feel light as air. It lifts us up and makes everything lovely. Look at Maslow and ask the question, What does the audience need? To feel light? To feel effortless? To see beauty? To know beauty is part of their community? To connect themselves to history and culture? To ensure their town has a cultural statement? These are needs. On Maslow's pyramid, you can see ballet in the top three levels: love and belonging, self-esteem, and self-actualization.

Harriett Lake was a great patron of the arts in my town of Orlando, Florida. She was quite a character. A fashionista before there was such a thing, she was famed for her hats, feathers, and lots of sparkle. She held a yearly "Harriett's Closet" charity event, where she essentially offered a rummage sale of her Gucci and Prada belongings to benefit charities she supported. Near the end of her life, she determined she would endow the Orlando Ballet with a beautiful new building that included space for rehearsals, classes, offices, and performances. Today, Harriett's Orlando Ballet Centre is a magnificent building on a lake with stunning two-story windows.

We've already talked about how arts, fashion, and fine dining are on the thrive tiers of the pyramid. But let's think about that a little deeper. Harriett's gift wasn't just a gift to the ballet. It was a gift to the city. A world-class ballet with an exceptional facility turns a surviving city into a thriving city. Is it possible Harriett could have seen her gift as essential to the survival of Orlando, a city that wants to be competitive in the market for high-paying jobs and company headquarters? I believe it's possible she saw the arts that way.

Wherever your brand sits on either pyramid, you can make a case for how your work helps people survive and thrive. When you connect with those elemental instincts, your target audience connects. For example, sometimes I tell my "Feliz Navidad, Mickey" story as a survival story about a woman with a child who needs a job. Sometimes I tell it as a thrive story—a woman with a creative eye who added value. It depends on what my audience needs. Both are true stories. I flip the script, depending on the audience.

When I tell the story about Henry's early years, I'm keenly aware not everyone can relate to our specific struggles. But when we apply the Story Formula, we can make any story relatable. What's universal about my child's struggles? My desire to help him self-actualize. Any parent can relate to that. Finding the universal in your story will connect with your audience's universal needs and wants. If my Henry story was just about the specifics—smearing feces into a CD-ROM of the family computer—well, that's a vivid picture. Perhaps too vivid. It must have the universal underpinning to connect with the listener and their struggles. Otherwise it's just a gross mommy story.

But again, without the specifics, a universal story can float too high above the heads of your audience. What if I had shared the story this way: "My son had autism, and it was a challenge. But with God's grace and through perseverance, we overcame many issues, and he's now living a rewarding life as a fully realized individual with autism." Well, that sounds very important, doesn't it? You wouldn't want your eyes to roll back in your head if I gave that speech from a podium at a fundraising dinner. You know it sounds important—but it's boring. You aren't going to get teary-eyed about how we "overcame issues through perseverance." You won't care or feel connected to my victory without the poop-filled CD-ROM.

Discover the survive-and-thrive of your story, and add rich detail. That's what makes every story compelling. That's what allows you to flip the script, move the details around, and apply the information of the story to different situations.

I tell my seminar attendees and I'm telling you: At their core, our stories are all stories of survival, and they're worth telling. Telling yours will help you thrive and someone else survive. By understanding who you're talking to and what they need at the moment, you can effectively flip the script and meet the moment.

Takeaways:
- ✓ Be willing to flip the script to meet the moment.
- ✓ Story is brain food. They train our brains to know we can overcome, and they show us how to do it.
- ✓ Stories help us survive and thrive. How does your story help your audience do this?
- ✓ Locate your story on Maslow's hierarchy of needs.

Chapter 3

Win the Crowd

Star of the Show

When I started my career as a professional actor, I joined a troupe of players called SAK Theatre that performed daily shows at what was then Epcot Center in Walt Disney World. We told our version of famous stories—*Romeo and Juliet* and *Robin Hood*—and original stories, such as *The Menace of Venice* and *The Big Bear Show*. These twenty-minute-long shows were performed by three actors who told the story and cast the main roles with audience members.

Most often, we picked unlikely people to play the parts—perhaps a grandma played Juliet and a grandpa played Romeo. It was quite a sight to see someone's nana with a flowing pink scarf on her head and someone else's gramps wearing a blue hero's cape, both of them running toward each other for a romantic embrace. The audience members were truly the stars of those shows.

This changed the paradigm of performing for me and for everyone who experienced those shows. I had expected to be an actor on a stage, all eyes on me in my wig, heavy makeup, and costume. With SAK's approach, the audience was the star of the show, and we were there to facilitate their experience. The entire story existed so we could make spectators the stars.

Turning myself into a servant so audience members could star in the show took a minute. It was a hard concept for me to grasp. But once I understood that no matter the role, my performance would always serve the audience, it changed my work and my life. That principle applied beyond the stage too. Connecting became more important than performing. Shared experiences trumped applause.

Most people talk about their organization's achievements. Whether via a website, a blog, a tweet, a meeting, or a speech, over and over, you tell the story of how you served, what you made, or the strength of your impact. You do it to woo your audience. But that begs the question: Is your story really about you? What if you're actually there to facilitate a story that makes your audience the star of the show?

Your story is about your audience. I know this may seem backward. You might be thinking, "No, our story is about our organization, and we're connecting with our audience." But in order to connect with your audience, your story must, in fact, be about your audience. Remember how your story is meant to be universal so anyone can relate to it?

Here's the secret truth. Your audience doesn't care if you survive and thrive. They care if *they* do. Do you remember the scene in *Gladiator* when Maximus meets with his mentor, the former gladiator who now runs the games? It follows the scene where Maximus wins a gladiator game in a bloody match and angrily yells at the crowd, "Are you not entertained?" His mentor, Proximo, tells him the crowd was not entertained. He goes on to explain that in order for Maximus to win his freedom, he needs to become beloved by the crowd. To do that, he needs to turn the blood sport into entertainment. The scene ends with Maximus saying, "I will win the crowd."

That's our job. We must win the crowd. We might wish we could demand our audience buy our goods and services. We might want to send a pledge form to everyone we know who watches our show and insist they donate. It might be easier if it all worked that way. But it doesn't. For our audience to donate to our cause or believe they need our goods and services, we must win them over.

Here's why.

I mentioned my son has autism. He's in his twenties now, and since he was around ten, I've asked him one question over and over: "What are you thinking about?" His answer is always the same. He joyfully raises his arms above his head and declares, "I'm thinking about me!" Come to think of it, that's what I'm thinking about too. I'm thinking about me! I'm thinking about me, even when I ask him the question. It's me who wants to know what he's thinking, so I can feel better about me!

The same is true for your customers, your audience, your clients, your donors, and your community. They aren't thinking about you. They don't want to hear about you. They want to hear about themselves. Every one of us wants that. We're thinking about ourselves. If my son asked me what I'm thinking about, if I was truthful, I'd raise my hands over my head and say, "I'm thinking about me!"

Your story is actually about your audience's survival. Again, they don't care if *you* survive and thrive. They care if *they* do. Think about the people who buy or use your services. What do they want? What are they in need of? What "want" do they have that makes them willing to get up and get it from you? Prove to them you can help them survive and/or thrive, and you'll win the crowd.

The Hero's Motivation

A friend of mine attended McDonald's Hamburger University in the '80s. He learned the company operated from the need to be flexible and to keep its audience's needs front and center. They had no idea what kind of food people would be eating in the year 2000, but whatever it was, they knew McDonald's would be serving it.

Did anyone who grew up eating cheeseburgers in the '70s ever imagine McDonald's would sell yogurt, salads, and frappes? No way. But they do. The audience had the need, so McDonald's menu provided for that need. If McDonalds still only sold those little cheeseburgers and fries, the company would be struggling now. In the 2020s, people eat low carbs and keto. They count WW points. McDonald's updated its menu because its customers are the stars of their show. The customers' wants and needs drive the business.

Using the classic story of the hero's journey, you can determine a character's wants and needs. In the hero's journey, we meet a character, our hero. This character has a strong want. You may have heard the actor cliché, "What's my motivation?" It may sound silly, and we've made it sound like a diva thing, but it's actually an important bit of information for an actor to have. To know how to play a character, you need to know what they want. Every actor looks for what their character wants and needs in order to drive a scene forward.

As a business leader, you have likely taken courses that talked about core values and intentions. It's very similar. Your intention drives your behavior. In a story, the hero's intention— their want—leads them to act. People don't do things unless they want to, and the want has to be strong enough for them to get up off a couch and go get it. In the hero's journey, the hero must want something or there's no reason for the quest. They must be willing to go get it.

Think of your favorite movie hero, like Harry Potter, Luke Skywalker, or Cinderella. Use a child's favorite movie, like *The Wizard of Oz* or *Moana*. Use your favorite to outline the hero's journey and find a character's want. Then you can apply it to your storytelling.

Drama Is Conflict

The next step in the hero's journey is a problem. Typically, a want comes from a problem. You aren't in Kansas anymore, and you want to go home. You're stuck on a desert planet at your uncle's farm, but you want to be a Jedi. You're sitting in cinders, but you want to go to the ball. In the hero's journey, there must be a problem. You want something because that thing solves a problem and overcomes an obstacle.

Drama is conflict. Daniel doesn't take karate from Mr. Miyagi in the original *Karate Kid* if he isn't bullied at his new school. He doesn't want or need to get up off the couch if he's not being bullied. Insert your chosen movie example here. What does the main character want, and what conflict is keeping them from getting that need met?

When you craft a story, look for trouble. When I'm working a story, I imagine John Wayne from *True Grit* saying to me, "Young fella, if you're lookin' for trouble, I'll accommodate ya." His voice helps me find the conflict. Where's the drama? Where's the conflict? If you can't find trouble, go back to the hero. What do they want? That's where the trouble is. Want and trouble go together. Listen for John Wayne asking you, "You lookin' for trouble, pardner?" Why yes, sir, I am.

If Dorothy just put Toto on a leash, that would be the end of the story. She doesn't do that because she doesn't want to. She wants Toto to run free. She wants to run free too. But they can't because they're stuck in Kansas, hemmed in by the prairie and mean ol' Miss Gulch. There's your trouble.

Drama is conflict, but in my experience this often becomes an issue for the people in charge. "No, no, we don't want any drama," you might hear a CEO or board member say. "We don't want to point out trouble." I've been told this enough that I've learned my lesson. Every compelling story I've pitched has been shut down when I've brought up conflict, drama, and problems. Just the mention of anything negative makes many decision makers wince.

The problem, though, is that a hero doesn't win if there's not a conflict to overcome. So look for trouble—just maybe don't bring it up to the board. Find it, get it in there, and use it for good.

The reason you need trouble is simple. Trouble is universal, and we can all relate to it. Every marketing campaign you've ever connected with included conflict. Really, it did! Nike's famous "Just Do It" campaign is a great example. Why would you need to be told to "Just Do It" if there wasn't something holding you back or in your way? The problem Nike solved was our reticence to get out on the field. It was our fear, our laziness, and our lack of interest in exercise or sports. Whatever your problem with exercise, that conflict is addressed with Nike's statement: "Just Do It."

"Just Do It" is a compelling call to action. In the hero's journey, that's often referred to as a call to adventure, which comes to the hero through someone known as the guide. This is a character who leads the hero on their journey. It's Mr. Miyagi. Glinda the Good. Dumbledore. The Fairy Godmother. Obi-Wan Kenobi.

The guide is key to the hero's journey because they give the hero the plan. Wax on; wax off. Go to the Emerald City. Harry, you're a wizard. Be back by midnight. Use the Force, Luke. The plan offered to the hero by the guide is a big idea that charges up the hero character. "Yeah! That's what I want! That will solve everything."

Once the hero knows where they need to go on their quest, their next question is how. Here comes the launch to their journey, the call to adventure that outlines the plan. Follow the yellow brick road. Here's your letter to Hogwarts School of Witchcraft and Wizardry. We need to get these droids to the resistance. The call comes with a question: Will you go? Heroes do go, because they have a want, a need, and a problem.

The journey begins, and there are many dangers along the way. Those challenges are your plot points. Finally, the story ends in victory—yay! Daniel wins the tournament. Dorothy and Toto get back home. Harry and his friends defeat He Who Must Not Be Named. The glass slipper fits. Or it all ends in tragedy (see Shakespeare).

This formula for the hero's journey isn't found just in fictional stories. You can also see it in marketing campaigns. Going back to "Just Do It," do a Google search for the original ad. In that 1988 commercial, the camera finds eighty-year-old Walt Stack jogging across the Golden Gate Bridge. He tells us he runs seventeen miles every morning. As he jogs along, he even gently jokes with us: "People ask me how I keep my teeth from chattering in the winter time." Cut to his feet running in a pair of Nikes. "I leave 'em in my locker," he says. Then the black screen with white lettering: "Just Do It."

Walt is our Obi-Wan giving us a plan. Just do it. Just get out there. He even tells us how he does it—jogs every morning, leaves his teeth in his locker. He shows us how to do it too— wear your Nikes, jog along at whatever pace you can.

Using the hero's journey in your storytelling will help your story connect with your target audience's wants and problems. I have a want to be like Walt, getting out there, enjoying my life, living robustly until I'm eighty, moving at my own pace. I have a want to be like Harry Potter, where the things that make me odd or different turn out to be gifts—indeed, a gift that saves the world. The want goes back to the Story Formula: "Universal so we relate. Specific so we care." I can relate to the hero's universal want, even if I can't relate to the specific needs in their story. The specifics are what keep my interest and make me care.

Everyone wants to take the hero's journey along with the character. That's what keeps us on the edge of our seats. What will happen? How will it turn out? That's true even when we know the ending. Think of the based-on-real-events movies you've watched. There's a list of them I'll drop everything to watch. *Argo. Captain Phillips. Hidden Figures. Molly's Game.* Anything about World War II. Do I have a problem? Maybe. I rewatch these movies because it's soothing to my brain to go through the journey. I know how they end—that makes it safe for me to go on the journey. I know the characters have a want, just like I do, and I get to experience how they grab hold of the plan and overcome obstacles. I want to experience their victory over a problem to remind myself that I can experience victory over my problem too.

Hero and Guide

It might seem that you should make your business the hero of your story. However, to be the hero of a story, you must have a problem that needs solving. If you make your company the hero, then you would be constantly in a position of weakness. You would be the one who's on a journey, the one who's meeting obstacles along the way.

Take a look at the heroes from all the films we've talked about. They have one thing in common. Do you see it? They're a hot mess. They're in need and in a vulnerable state. That's why they need to take a journey! Why did the chicken cross the road? To get to the other side. The hero needs to get to the other side of this road.

When you share your story from the hero position, you put yourself in the place of the person who needs help. Would you hire Episode I Luke Skywalker? No way. No one wants to be around that guy. Except for one person: Obi-Wan Kenobi. The guide.

This is what our acting troupe understood all those years ago, when we were doing shows on the streets at Epcot. The audience was the star of the show, and we were the storytellers. They were the hero, and we were there to guide them on their way. I've seen many other acts attempt to pull audience members out of their seats and stick them in a show, and it usually fails. An individual does not want to get out of their seat and become part of the show. The only thing that compels them is if it becomes clear that they *need* to be part of the show. We need them in order to succeed. We have a plan, one that works every time, and we will guide them. We won't let them fail or embarrass themselves in front of their family. We know the story. We know where they're going, and we're going to make them look great getting there.

If you need help with this concept of the hero and a guide, Donald Miller's book *Building a StoryBrand* is a must-have tool. He created a framework for your brand with this position: audience as the hero; company as the guide. This concept will change your life. I highly recommend his book for understanding the concept as a framework.

The bottom line is, once again, you need to flip the script. Your client (or donor or customer or audience) has a need, and you have the solution. You're already the guide in your business. As a speaker, you're there to guide those listening. You're there to share your insights about a problem they're having. You're giving them a plan and calling them to action.

As an individual, I know you've been striving to be the hero of your own story. Go ahead and try being the Fairy Godmother instead. Wouldn't it be great if you were the one with the magic wand? If you were the one with the peace and confidence in how this story ends? In your area of expertise, you actually are that person. You're the one with a plan to move your audience forward on their journey.

Flipping this script solves a multitude of problems. First, you get to explore all kinds of conflict in your storytelling because you're the one with the solution. You can share the weaknesses, the needs, and the wants of the hero because you have a plan. Your CEOs will never notice. They'll have no clue you added drama and need to your story. They'll feel like Glinda the Good—peaceful, centered, and floating above the conflict in a big, pink bubble. Which is great, because that's who you are.

Needs and Wants

Now that you know who the hero is, you can use a quick worksheet to discover your audience's wants and needs. Think of your target audience and ask: What do they want, and what is keeping them from getting that?

You can practice with any movie or book that you know. Find the universal themes that anyone can relate to and what specific problems make us care. Then pair what you've found with the character's wants and needs.

Let's take two movies here and run them through the worksheet.

I Am Legend

Universal theme so we relate: We all have a part to play. We have a destiny.

Specific problem so we care: Zombie virus is destroying humanity, New York City in particular.

Need: I need to find a cure.

Want: I want to fix this.

Cinderella

Universal theme so we relate: I'm being overlooked.

Specific problem so we care: Evil stepmother has me doing grueling housework.

Need: I need to go to the ball.

Want: I want to be seen and valued.

Do you notice the difference between their needs and wants? The need is usually the tangible, specific problem right in front of the character. The want is the character's internal motivation, the hurt that's at the core of who they are, driving their behaviors.

Now it's your turn. Boil down any of the stories you're working on this way:

Universal theme so we relate:
Specific problem so we care:
Need:
Want:

Look for the trouble, find it, and then share your beautiful plan for how to get out of it. Your listeners are the ones on the journey, but you've already arrived. The conclusion of the story is that your work is good for the community or that your product can serve them well or that your services can benefit their lives. When you share a story that helps your audience feel they're on a hero's journey and that you have a solution that gets them to victory, you'll win the crowd.

Statement to Story

One of the groups I work with takes potential clients and donors on a tour of their facility. Before our story workshops, they called them the "doorknob tours." They would go from room to room, telling people, "This is what we do here," "This is what happens here," "This is what the students work on here." Since our sessions, they've changed the doorknob tours into "story tours." At each doorknob, they now tell the story of someone in their program who experienced a victory because of the work done in the program right in that room. They flipped the script.

Another time, I led a session for an organization that helps children in the hospital by housing and serving their families. They had a straightforward "What We Do" statement, which was "Keeping families with sick children together and near the care and resources they need." That's a beautiful statement, and it's also a fact—it's what they do.

But so what? If I'm not a family with a sick child, then why do I care? What does this have to do with me? Why should I donate or drop dimes in the box? Why should I buy a ticket to the gala or donate a silent auction item? It doesn't seem to impact me at all.

We wanted to play with that statement and create a story based on the facts. In our statement-to-story exercise, we started with the problem they solved for the community by examining the journey a family takes in their care:

- Arrive at the airport with a sick child.
- Rent a car.
- Drive to a hotel near the hospital.
- Grandparents arrive.
- Family care given in shifts.
- Mom sits by the bedside.
- Dad takes the other two kids for breakfast.
- Dad finds something for the kids to do.
- Mom comes back and needs a nap, then a cup of coffee.
- Dad heads to the hospital.
- The other kids need lunch.

What does all this do to a community? We've got people coming into the city confused, worried, worn out, and in search of resources for the basic essentials of life. They don't know the roads. They don't know where the 7-Eleven is, or the Starbucks, or the playground—and they're too tired to figure it out. We, as a community, need someone who can take them where they need to go. We need people to get them settled so they can focus on their child's healing. We need a way for them to transition seamlessly into our community.

We thought about universal themes by considering who we are as a community. What do we, as a community, want to be our image? We're compassionate. We have amazing specialty hospitals, and we want people to take advantage of these resources. We want people to feel welcome when they're here. This is a nice town, but no one will feel that way if they're wandering the aisles of Walmart, trying to find everything they need to make lunches in a motel.

We looked again at the statement: "Keeping families with sick children together and near the care and resources they need." How could we meet the need of the moment with a donor by flipping the script and sharing a story version of this statement?

Here was our result: "Families with sick or injured children are overwhelmed. They can't handle the logistics of daily life. We provide them a place to stay near the hospital. We give them a good cup of coffee in the morning. We've got lunch covered, and we do the dishes. There's a playground for the other kids. A quiet spot for Mom to take a nap. Our homes gives caretakers what they need so they can focus on the full health of their family—and we do it all with your help."

If a donor hears this story, they can't help but feel themselves the star of it. These families have a need, and so does the donor—to be part of this kind of loving care in their city. They may not be the one making the coffee for the family, but they can be the one to fund it and ensure it happens. By creating specific pictures of what care looks like, the donor can picture their place in this story.

We envisioned the organization as the wise guide who could see the family's needs and journey and knew how to provide a plan for their triumph. We also positioned the donor as the winner of the bigger victory. They would be the one to make this success possible. Then we wrapped up with the solution: "This is what happens, donor, if you enter our story."

When you're talking with a donor, a county commissioner, or a volunteer, you can't spout a brand statement. They'll think you're some sort of bizarre brand robot. When you're being interviewed for a profile in a city magazine as one of the most influential people in town, you need to meet the moment with a story that conveys your organization's ability to help people survive and thrive. This tool of turning statements into story helps you get there.

Beyond the Origin Story

Most companies start out of a need or a passion. Someone is struggling with something and can't get the answers they need, so they start a nonprofit. Or you have a passion and a talent, so you launch a digital start-up. You've got a message, so you write a book and become a speaker.

When startups begin with a dream and a crisis, the origin story of the organization can end up becoming the brand story. That is usually great—until it's not great. Until it's the only story you've told over and over again. Until it's the story your staff tells with too much regularity. I call it the "we started in a garage" story. It's on pretty much every website.

The executive director's story of "crisis to dream to success-ful business" is really interesting—for a memoir or *CBS Sunday Morning* profile. It is not enough to get members, entice clients, or solicit donations. At that moment, the story you're telling needs to be about the people you're telling it to.

Let me give you an example. OCA is "a special place for special needs." Its name stands for Opportunity, Community, Ability, and it started with a passion and a need. Our school's special needs PE coach, Silvia Haas, was worried about her son and other kids she taught who were on the autism spectrum. She worried about what would happen to them after they became adults. She worried about who would take care of them when we're gone.

There were no organizations in our area that helped our kids thrive. You had to move up north for that, and many families did. But a big group of us didn't want to retire from Florida to upstate New York. After all, we had given up driving in snow about twenty years before. We had the need for services, and we wanted them in Orlando. Silvia Haas and three of her friends, whom she calls the founding sisters, started an organization at first designed to get our kids active after school.

They held Special Olympics soccer and track. Later, as programs grew, she dreamed of creating a place where our kids could work, live, and play. She became CEO of OCA, an organization that serves elementary school kids after class and in summer camps. There's an adult vocational program. There's a theater company. There are dance classes, music classes, and even a vision for a village.

The origin story is worth telling—by me. By magazines and TV stations looking for feel-good stories. But the origin story isn't the one OCA needs to tell over and over again to different audiences. They need to tell the story of the donor or the community or any other "me" who might cross their path, telling the story of what they want and how they get it, thanks to the existence of this organization.

Let's use our tools and see if we can go beyond the origin story. Let's look at OCA from the perspective of two audiences they serve: caretakers of individuals with autism and the Central Florida community. How could they move beyond the origin story to help their different audiences survive and thrive?

Audience #1: Caretakers

Universal: Health and safety. Desire to see their child safe and well.

Specific: Single mom. Seven-year-old with autism, diagnosed at two years old.

Need: You're deep in the weeds of figuring out what to do. You've got the diet down and some basic behavior plans at home. You've even got a school program that works. Now what? What do you do about his future? What about this summer? You're too exhausted to even think about it.

Want: To know that their child belongs. To know their child's abilities have value.

Story: We start with an after-school program that builds social skills and physical fitness and develops your child's unique abilities. It also gives you a break. We add social skills on the weekends and camps in the summer. We develop a community for your child that leads to an adult program to which he can contribute his abilities. Your child has opportunities to grow his abilities in a community that will be with him the rest of his life.

Audience #2: Community

Universal: Health and safety of all citizens. Also look higher up on Maslow's pyramid to esteem and recognition through leaving a legacy.

Specific: Central Florida.

Need: There are very few special needs school programs and almost no post-school adult programs. Now you've got these families living here, and since 2018, one in forty-four of them has a kid with autism. That number keeps climbing, and with a population of just over eight million, in about twenty years you're going to have a serious issue—more than a hundred thousand adults with autism flooding the system.

Want: To have a cultural identity as a city and region that's inclusive, creative, and, well, cool.

Story: We want those adults with autism to contribute to Central Florida. Central Florida would become known as an innovator for inclusion and a place that nurtures people with autism. You could have a beautiful village center where people with autism live, rather than a bunch of shelter homes. You could walk your dog down to Axum Coffee in Winter Garden, sit outside, and be greeted by Jimmy, an adult with autism. He knows your order because he knows you. It feels good to both of you to be known and seen. The area is a cool, interesting place to live, where people with disabilities aren't hidden away but are active and helpful community members. At OCA, we build their work skills, help them navigate social situations, and provide a place for them to work, live, and play.

More Than One Audience

At first glance, you're likely to think your target audience is the person who buys your stuff. But most businesses end up with two audiences they must appeal to: the ones who use their goods and services, and the ones who help fund their goods and services. Nonprofits have participants and donors. Entrepreneurs have clients and investors.

Understanding two audiences is clearest in the nonprofit sector, as you can see from the example above. I'll tell you what I told one of my nonprofit clients, a man who was going to present the story of the largest homeless service organization in Orlando to a group of wealthy donors at a breakfast in Winter Park. In our town, Orlando is like Los Angeles and Winter Park is like Beverly Hills—a very upscale neighborhood. I met him in the lobby of the fanciest hotel and he was sweating. He told me he was too nervous and would need to read his speech. I told him it was fine, of course, if he read his speech, but I didn't want him to lose his spark. He is a naturally gifted speaker. His story, that of being homeless and now serving as a director at the organization and overseeing several departments, is inspiring.

A woman with Gucci shoes interrupted us to invite us into the dining room to start the program. I grabbed his arm, "Look, I know how you feel. My dad was a navy captain, and I feel out of place here. That woman's shoes are the price of my car payment. But these people want to hear your story. They have money they need to share, and they want to know about you. You're the expert here. Tell them what to do to help their city." He told his story and received a grant for more than twenty-five thousand dollars that morning.

His story was just as inspiring when he told it another time to a group of men who arrived at the shelter the day before the last hurricane blew through Central Florida. Same story; different audience and purpose. One audience had the means to support the organization, and one audience needed the organization's support.

Take that same bit of advice I gave him—"Tell them what to do to help their city"—and apply it to your different audiences. You need to be able to adjust your story to meet their specific needs. If you are making an individual sale or pitching your company to a sponsor, they have different needs and a different way of using your product or service to meet that need. Tell them what to do to overcome the issue in front of them.

This can be a bit mind-bending if you're an individual rather than a business. Maybe you're a speaker giving a talk to a large convention, an actor trying to land a gig, or a graphic designer interviewing for a job. You might be tempted to lean into your origin story too, but you need to resist that temptation as much as a business does. The question is: How do you engage your audience when the product is you? Let's work two examples and see how this can apply to your situation.

First, imagine you are a speaker with expertise in customer service giving a speech at the annual convention of the National Apartment Association. Your worksheet for an audience of apartment and condo managers might look like this:

Universal: You matter.

Specific: National Apartment Association convention. Ten thousand members. High-rise complexes. Apartment communities. Gathering places. Pools. Workout rooms. Broken garage doors. Backed-up sinks. Dog-walk areas.

Need: A thankless job in the face of a never-ending stream of complaints, repairs, and unpaid rent.

Want: To believe they have value and their work has value.

Story: Go beyond merely giving them three strategies for providing great customer service. Help them know they matter. They deserve those three strategies because their work should be rewarding. The strategies provide them with a stronger sense of self that will help them weather challenging conditions.

Now let's imagine you're an actor going into an audition. How do you speak to what is likely an audience of one, the casting director? What are their needs and wants? How can you meet them there?

Universal: The satisfaction of doing their job well.

Specific: Theater. Studio. Folding chairs in a hallway. People holding their photos. A single camera with a blinking red light. Stale coffee. A row of competitors just outside the door.

Need: A specific role to fill. One actor to hire. Pressure to get it right in a sea of hopefuls they see every day.

Want: To feel good about their find. A pat on the back from the director or producer.

Story: Create a winning environment—peaceful or energetic—that makes the casting director feel good in the middle of a difficult day. Give the best read that you can. Then follow up with content for social media that showcases your gifts as an actor for the casting director's later reference. Through you, the casting director has found an actor who makes it easy. The online material is there to back up their decision to hire you now or in the future.

This second example can be a tough one because you can't guarantee you're going to book a job as an actor—as is true with any professional going into a job interview or any sales executive pitching a client. You have no idea what factors will drive their ultimate decision.

When I was a casting director at the *American Idol* show at Walt Disney World, I saw up to fifty young singers a day. I told my kids—or more accurately, their parents—that as an entertainer, they should expect to have anywhere from ten to twenty-five auditions a year to book one or two jobs. This can be scary for a parent, who has likely not had more than ten job interviews and probably two or three jobs in their entire career.

Having a mindset geared toward serving your audience is healthier than a "you need to hire me" mentality. Use the hero's journey and be the guide in your interview setting, rather than the hero who needs to win. The need to win presents a feeling that whomever you're pitching needs to lose. This is true with any offer you make, be it a sales email or a donor meeting.

Using the audition scenario, the actor could make a tiny shift from "I can be great in this role" (or, as every actor in *A Chorus Line* sings, "Please God, I need this job") to "This moment is about *you,* casting director, finding the right person for your boss. I'm a good actor—a great actor, really—and I can be great in this role and many others you have to cast. I may not be the answer to your problem today, but I'm the answer to your larger problem. You need actors you can count on. I'll be there for you."

This is similar to a company sending out emails in a campaign to sell a product. You can use this shift in your intention and see results. When you make that tonal shift from "This is about *me* and how you can solve *my* problem" (I need this sale) to "This is about *you* and here's how I solve *your* problems," you'll create a lasting relationship with a customer. Try it in your next email campaign. Make the tone "I'm here for you with this offer. I've got the solution to your problems." Move away from them being the solution to your needs. Instead, become the solution to their needs.

Remember, the audience is the star of your show. Make the story about them. Make it universal and specific, and you'll win the crowd.

Sticky Stories

I hear you resisting all this. "This doesn't apply to us or our organization," you might be saying. "That won't work for our product." Work the Story Formula, and you'll begin to see not only how your story is about your audience's universal wants and desires, but also how adding specifics lights up their brains and make them stick to you and your brand.

Specific details are what make a story "sticky." In his book *The Tipping Point,* Malcolm Gladwell defined the Stickiness Factor as the quality that compels people to pay close, sustained attention to a product, concept, or idea.[6] In so doing, Gladwell doomed all marketing and communications professionals to hear this question from now until kingdom come: "Yeah, but is it sticky?"

By Gladwell's definition, to make a story sticky, it needs to include something that a reader will be compelled to pay attention to. What was it in Oprah's story we couldn't shake? Oh, that's right—linoleum. Sticky.

Let's look again at my holiday story. Why would I tell you the "Feliz Navidad, Mickey" story? None of you has been an actor at a theme park in Mexico, opening a new show for the holidays. But I started by telling you I was an actor that was "shipped to different countries." I was an employee, and I was sent to do something based on the company's needs. You've been in that situation. Then I told you about the logistical problems of my job—kids to wrangle, a well-known brand I needed to make look good. I'm giving you a playbook for overcoming your own problems at work.

I'm not telling you about the time I got to be on a stage at Walt Disney World doing a holiday show for adoring fans. I know a couple hundred people who know what it feels like to be onstage at Walt Disney World, and believe me, it's as fabulous as it sounds. But if you've never experienced it, it will mean nothing to you. That would be about me and my fabulous experience. But this story is about you and how you need to connect with your audience. The story *must* be about you for you to connect. That's what makes a sticky story.

Look again at Oprah's Golden Globe speech. It's an acceptance speech for a lifetime achievement award. Pretty much the topic is all about her. You can't get around that—except she did. She began with "When I was a little girl" as an invitation. Me and you, we're the same. We were little kids once. She takes us on a journey that, in this section, wraps with, "It is not lost on me that at this moment, there are some little girls watching as I become the first black woman to be given this same award." It's about us.

She could have given the speech so many give: "Thank you, thank you! I want to start by thanking my manager—we've been through a lot, huh? And of course, my agent and publicist—you're always there when I need you. My bestie, Gayle, is here today. What a trip this has been! And of course, Stedman, my rock. When I was first starting out in broadcasting, blah blah blah blah blah." You can feel the barriers go up. Thank you—to a very specific group of people that doesn't include any of us. "We've been through a lot." Well, that's two of you. We're not part of this at all. We're spectators.

Instead, she opens the window and we can see ourselves. We can be a little girl sitting on the linoleum floor. We had hopes and dreams then, and we have hopes and dreams now. She's giving us a playbook for our story. She turns us from spectators to stars.

One more thing about heroes. They have a very short shelf life. Once their problem is solved, they're out. Who wants to hear about their happily ever after? No one. Not even straight to video. You can be the Fairy Godmother, waving your wand and making people's dreams come true for a much longer time. So do that. Be the Fairy Godmother.

Takeaways:

- ✓ Your audience cares about their own need to survive and thrive—not yours.
- ✓ A person's want leads them to act. What does your audience want?
- ✓ A want comes from a problem. What problem does your audience face? Look for the trouble.
- ✓ Your audience is the hero; your company is the guide.
- ✓ Do the work of turning your statements into stories.
- ✓ Go beyond your origin story.
- ✓ Keep your story sticky with specifics.

Part II
Develop

Chapter 4

Open the Window

Cross Country in a Blue Dodge Dart

When I was seven years old, my dad drove me across the country from his post in Vancouver, Washington, to our next home in Northern Virginia. It was 1972. There was no iPad, smartphone, or TV built into the headrest of the minivan. There was a blue Dodge Dart with vinyl seats, a lap belt, a built-in AM/FM radio, and no air conditioning. Depending on where we were, the radio stations drifted in and out.

The first day of our trip, my dad put me in the back seat, next to our dog, Peppy, and said, "I'm going to tell you a story from here to Virginia. I'm going to tell you the story of the West." Off we went. When we stopped to stand in the wagon ruts in Wyoming, he told me the story of my three-times-great-grandmother, who had traveled the Oregon

Trail in a covered wagon. Lulu was seven years old in 1872, a century's distance from me.

I thought about Lulu as I headed east in the blue Dart. Every landscape brought the history of the place and the people into focus. I heard about the people of the Great Plains, like the Blackfoot and the Crow. I heard about the buffalo and the railroads. We saw natural landmarks, like Chimney Rock and Yellowstone. We stopped at the Battle of Little Bighorn and I heard the story of Custer and Sitting Bull. Stories about explorers Sacagawea and Lewis and Clark. Stories about outlaws, like the Hole in the Wall Gang and Butch Cassidy and the Sundance Kid.

Telling stories did more than distract a fidgety child. The stories connected me to the land I was seeing, the culture of each place, and the events that happened there. They also connected me to the storyteller, my dad. Everything was a story, and I was now part of the story.

What my dad knew was that to entertain a little girl, and likely himself, on a long car ride, he could tell stories. What he didn't know was that by starting the trip with the declaration "I'm going to tell you a story from here to Virginia," he opened a window and I climbed right in.

You open the window to your brand by inviting your audience into your story. You now know what your story is really about (surviving and thriving) and why your story really matters (it's universal and specific) and who your story is really about (your audience). Because of that, you can create stories your audience will remember.

Telling a great story is about painting a picture your audience can't shake. The way to achieve that is to leave room for them to paint themselves into your picture. When an audience sees themselves in your story, you have won the crowd. The way to invite them in is to hook them early on in the story.

And Then What?

An exercise I use in my live workshops shows how compelling the basic fact of a story can be. In the exercise, the group splits into pairs, with each pair having a Person A and Person B. Person A starts a story—a very basic, boring story. We usually start with, "On my way home from the seminar today." The goal is to imagine and then recount what might happen on the way home: "I got in my car, drove to the gas station, stopped to fill up, and went inside and got a Diet Sprite." Just the facts, ma'am.

Person B is tasked with adding made-up facts to Person A's boring story. They might say, "And a clown car pulled up next to me."

Person A now needs to incorporate that new fact into the story, continuing with this added information: "A clown car pulled up next to me, and a hundred clowns got out of the car. They started making balloon animals and taught me how to make one shaped like a dog."

Then Person B, continuing to add made-up facts to the story, might say: "Then a plague of frogs dropped from the sky." So Person A continues: "When the plague of frogs dropped from the sky..."

You see how it goes. We do that for about a minute, and then they switch.

Every time I lead this exercise, I ask which role is harder. Those who play Person A usually report some nerves from the stress of incorporating new information on the spot, but it is most often those who play Person B who report having the hardest time. Why? Because they usually forget to interrupt Person A. They're too interested in what's going to happen next—even in the super boring story, when Person A was just stopping to get gas. Those playing Person B, just by listening to a very boring story, start thinking, "I wonder what she's going to do after she gets gas—oh, right, I need to come up with something to add to the story."

That's the power of a story.

If you've taken a writing class, you've likely learned about "the hook." Finding a way to hook your reader is key to your success in creating that bond with them. Some screenwriters call it a story loop.

It's a challenge to find the hook, but the simplicity of opening a story loop captures your audience—even if it's the simple recounting of activities after a seminar:

"I got in my car."

"Yes, yes—and then what?"

"I went to the 7-Eleven."

"Really? And then what?"

"I got gas and decided I deserved a Slurpee."

"Yes! You did!"

We can't get out of a story loop once we're in it. Have you ever watched a movie you didn't enjoy all the way to the end, just to find out what happened? Or continued with a book you weren't into (or maybe flipped to the last page) because you had to know how it ended? The hook or story loop opens a window. We're on the outside of something, and when the window opens, we look in and want to know what's happening.

Simply put, a hook grabs the reader's attention and makes them want to keep reading. Stories that start with a strong hook open that window through which the audience enters. The hook leaves us asking the question "And then what?"

Elizabeth Gilbert's *Eat Pray Love* opens with this sentence: "I wish Giovanni would kiss me." Well, now, so do we. We need to know: Why does she want him to kiss her? Why does she want to be kissed? Who is Giovanni? Why doesn't he want to kiss her?

Oh my! And then what?

A famous trick writers use to get into the habit of creating great hooks is to open the first page of any best-selling book. Read the first line or the first paragraph. That will help you see how story loops open.

More than becoming a great writer, you need to know that even a very basic story leaves us asking the question "And then what?" Any writer, no matter their experience, no matter if they're writing the first chapter of the great American novel or copy for a LinkedIn post, can hook a reader by opening a story loop.

Third Person

Another one of the exercises in my story workshops has participants introduce themselves using third person. Often these events are attended by individuals from different organizations who haven't worked together before, so introductions are important. We need to know who each other is. In fact, we're dying to know. No one can focus or participate while the question "Who is that?" niggles in the back of their minds.

Before the seminar, I ask participants to write a paragraph that introduces themselves in third person and to bring it with them. They pass their introduction to someone they haven't met, and the stranger reads the third-person introduction to the group. Each person hears their story told by someone from the outside.

I do this exercise because we're all so very close to our mission statements. We're inside our organizations. Often we don't know how to tell our own stories. We get caught up in the details. We leave out the most compelling parts because we think no one would care. In a sense, we're already hooked into our own story, and we can't always see what will hook someone else.

How might using the third person help you tell your organization's story? How might it help you craft your elevator pitch? Imagine a reader a hundred years from now reading that paragraph about you, your company, or your product. Telling it from the point of view of an overhead drone can help remove all the emotions you have surrounding your story. How much stress and pressure do you carry about crafting your elevator pitch? Write it in third person, like you're describing the pitch of your best friend's product or business. Then read it out loud. It sounds nice, right? See if third person can help unburden you from any fear, nerves, imposter syndrome, or shame that tries to take you down.

I struggle with being too close to my own story too—especially when I work with my son. Henry is in his twenties now and, as I've mentioned, has autism and is a talk show host. He's always been a talk show host. That's how he relates to the world. That's how he talks. As a good (stage) mother, I want to give him opportunities to use his gifts. We create videos, he speaks at events, and he has had his own talk show on YouTube and Facebook Live.

OCA, the organization I introduced in the last chapter, helped me raise Henry. Their executive director, Silvia, started *The OCA Show* at Henry's insistence. I don't know if you have someone with autism in your life, but repetition is a hallmark of the condition. When someone tells you every day at three thirty, "I'm the host of *The OCA Show* in syndication," you create a show, if just to get them to stop saying it. Because OCA and Silvia gave Henry this opportunity, whenever they need me or him, we're there. Could we send them a video of Henry talking about this or that program? Thanking the donors? Introducing Silvia at this fundraiser? Yes, yes, and yes.

My process is that I write Henry a script and shoot a video or rehearse for an event with him. Then I send Silvia every take of the video or hand him over to her before the live event. Why? Because I can't edit Henry. I can't coach him live. I can't choose the best take for the organization. I too often delete the one with the most heart because I want him to be perfect. I look at one video and get nervous he didn't hit his mark or we didn't get the message across or he's flapping his hands and displaying too many autistic behaviors. I cut the talk show patter he's added. Sometimes you can even hear me off camera saying, "Stay on script!" I get nervous and afraid of showing our soft underbelly.

But most of the time, his Henryisms are the best part. The funny things Henry does and says are part of my everyday existence, and I don't always see them as special. They're regular to me.

Silvia and her team also know Henry, but they aren't as connected to him as I am. When they see him speak, they see what an audience sees. I'm too tangled up with who he is (and who I am to him) to be able to tell what an audience will see and experience. Silvia can view our attempt in the third person, if you will.

Third person is a great way to disengage and float above the story. Trying on a different point of view, like that of an author crafting a story rather than being the subject of that story, can help you see different angles on your story. You'll see how to hook a reader by placing yourself in the position of a reader.

Stepping back gives you a new view of your story. It takes you out of the energy of the must-do's and the agendas and the things you need right now and gives you a little breathing space. When you're coming up with your own elevator pitch, it's usually charged with an undercurrent of "I need this person to understand me so I can (fill in the blank)"—get a job, secure funding, make a network connection. When you flip it and craft your elevator pitch in third person, you remove all that demand and see the story from above.

Yes, Let's!

Your third-person narrative is there to give you a broader view, but it likely doesn't answer the question "And then what?" Even your simplest story can be as compelling as the boring version of what you did on the way home from the seminar if it answers the question "And then what?"

The way to get your story moving is through action. You'll hook your listeners or readers to the universal and specific of your story with action. Remember how, in chapter 2, we listed action verbs? Developing the action in your story requires more than just verbs. It actually requires movement.

A way to find action is to get up and move. The improv game "Yes, Let's!" is a group version of that famous improv rule "Yes, And." A group of three to five people take the stage. The audience offers a suggestion of a place to go. The individuals onstage then take turns making offers, too, about what the group can do together in that place. As each suggestion is offered, everyone in the group raises their arms above their heads and jubilantly cries, "Yes, let's!" Then they mime the suggested action.

A typical scene could go like this:

Suggested place: Beach
Morgan: Let's go to the beach!
All: Yes, let's!
Group runs to the beach.
Joel: Let's dig in the sand.
All: Yes, let's!
Group mimes digging in the sand.
Jonathan: I found a buried treasure chest. Let's open it.
All: Yes, let's!
Group pretends to open the chest.
Clare: It's pirate gold! Let's buy a ship and sail the seven seas.
All: Yes, let's!

And on and on it goes—except that when a group of inexperienced seminar participants gets together, the exercise usually looks like this:

Sam: Let's go to the beach!
All: Yes, let's!

All walk in a circle.
Annie: Let's drive there.
All: Yes, let's!
All walk in a circle.
Mark: Let's get some sunscreen.
All: Yes, let's!
All walk in a circle.

In the first example, a seasoned group of improvisors shows through action how they go to the beach. The story moves forward, and more things happen as a result of them actually going to the beach. Improvisors know they need to *do* something or a scene dies. They fling themselves on stage and start doing. That's what makes it interesting.

When novices first do this exercise, they tend to talk *about* doing something. No one ever gets to the beach. No one ever mimes an action. They all just wander in a circle. It's weird, but it happens pretty much every time I lead this exercise. I usually have to stop them and point out that, as a group, they're going in circles.

This is a handy metaphor for what happens when we don't use action in our sentences. The story circles around and around, and nothing happens. They talk about doing something, but by the time they get to the action, the listener or the reader is asleep.

Stories full of circles usually start out like this: "Well, you know, I really wanted to become an entrepreneur. I thought about it and thought about it from my cubicle, and I really wanted to make a move, but of course I was afraid. Oh, and my Aunt Lynn tried to have her own business, and that was a miserable failure, and my neighbor was a Mary Kay lady, and that's all I could think of, was that I would be like a Mary Kay lady without the pink Cadillac. So anyway, I finally got up the nerve to actually make a plan..." It could go on like this seemingly forever until the speaker finally says something like, "So then I booked a table at the Sunday farmer's market, baked my famous cookies, and sold out on my first day."

What's tricky about the story-in-circles habit is that it's filled with interesting and sensory detail. The storyteller loads it with pictures, but it's just not going anywhere. As a listener, you know that feeling where you're kind of interested because there are pictures that keep you listening, but you keep wondering, "Yeah, and then what?" You need both sensory detail and action to tell your story. Action is the secret to discovering which specific details to keep in your story.

When you leap in and do an action—say, mime digging in the sand—that's when the next action pops up. You see yourself digging, you see the sand, your arms move, and you "discover" a treasure chest. Action leads to discovery. Action moves you forward.

Improvisation follows a formula of "Offer, Yes, Action." Can you apply this to your story? Suggest an action in your story and then see where it goes. Write an action hero story about your organization. Take a staff member. Take a participant. What do they do? What action do they take? What action does that lead to next?

Let's take the example above of the entrepreneur and turn it into an action-driven story. They might tell the story like this: "I was sitting in my cubicle day after day, dreaming of becoming an entrepreneur. I was afraid because I'd seen failure up close when my Aunt Lynn tried to launch her own business. Finally, one lunch hour, I put in an application for a table at the local farmer's market. I got accepted, and I didn't even have a name for my business, a logo, or even much of an idea! But I did know that everyone at work always asked for my 'famous cookies' at every potluck. The farmer's market was three Sundays away, and I got to work making dozens of cookies. It was my start."

On a second draft, could we add some color, drill down into more specific details that add interest? Absolutely. The point is to create an outline based on verbs. In each sentence of this example, there's an action. The speaker does something. Those actions show you the shape of the story. Then you can go back to your "Specific so they care" list and pick out sensory details. I'd like to know what kind of cookies they were so I could smell them baking, wouldn't you?

This brings us to a word about drafts. It's a great temptation to block yourself before you get to the action. You think, "Oh, that will never work," and then you have a whole mental list of why it won't work. But to develop a great story, you need to have options—many options. Which means drafts—many drafts.

You remember drafts from school? They didn't get the final grade. My elementary school teacher told us to write "Sloppy Copy" at the top of our drafts when we handed them in. This reduced any expectation that what we were turning in would be anything but sloppy.

When you need a lot of stories—like, say, fifty-two a year so you can share one a week on Facebook—you can afford some sloppy copies. Try brainstorming story ideas with this formula of "Offer, Yes, Action." You don't have to use all the ideas you put forward—or any of them, actually. In brainstorming, just say yes to every offer and see how many ideas you can amass. Later you can choose the ideas you really want to work with.

You block the flow of action when you deny an offer. When that happens, you limit yourself to one or two options, and that's not enough room to develop many stories, or even one story. What if you were able to write a series of social media posts with the attitude of "Yes, Let's"? How many ideas for one-sentence stories could you come up with if you considered this formula of "Offer, Yes, Action"?

You open the window to your brand by inviting your audience into your story. If you want your story to be a sticky story, you need to leave a window open for the audience to invite themselves into the narrative. We talked about how the audience is the star of your show. As the storyteller, you invite your listener into the story by opening a loop.

It used to be painful for me to write something that wasn't the final draft. I didn't like sloppy copies. I wanted each piece to be great. The trouble is, the only way to get to the final destination is through. I now discover my story by doing, not by thinking about doing. It's amazing how much buried treasure you can find if you just start digging.

Takeaways:

✓ Telling a great story is about painting a picture your audience can't shake. Leave room for them to paint themselves into the picture.

Chapter 5

Find the Flow

Roots Run Deep

I once wrote a tour script for a new performing arts center in Orlando, Florida. Many of the lobby spaces showcased unique pieces of furniture that came from a shop called Washburn Imports. I know this because I went to high school with John Washburn, the owner of the store. He put a bar in his store where you could sit at the imported teak tables while drinking craft beer, so I was very familiar with the furniture.

Once I finished the script, docents were trained to give the tour. Months later, I revisited the tour and heard a guest admiring an imported side table made from the roots of a tree. The tour guide piped right up that those trees were once on the site of the performing arts center and that when they were cut down, the trunks were fashioned into coffee tables for the lobby.

Wow—now, that's a story!

The only trouble was, it wasn't the real one.

How did we get there? Easy.

During a tour months earlier, a guest had asked where the tables came from. "You know, I don't know," the tour docent started to say. Then the guests started their own conversation: "I wonder if they're from the trees that used to be here." "Remember that old oak tree that was on the corner?" Everyone started chatting casually about this idea, and it got lodged in the minds of the two volunteers, who then incorporated it into their tours going forward. This led to even more people adopting the story until it became a major plot point of the tour.

My preacher, Dr. Joel Hunter, once told a story about sheep that stuck with me. He said the reason sheep are often the main characters in Jesus's parables is because of how they get lost. Sheep don't run away. They don't head off on their own. They simply nibble their way lost. They go from one tuft of grass to the next, never looking up, until they are the lost sheep.

I often say that in telling our stories over and over, we too can nibble our way lost. I've trained many employees to tell the story of their brand, only to come back six months later to discover that, tuft by tuft, they'd nibbled their way lost from the facts.

I've done it in my own work as well. The first thing I do when writing a large project, like a book manuscript, is to create an outline on poster board. I stick it to the wall of my office so I can see the list of every story in the book. That's because when

I can't see the flow from above, I start reworking each little part once I'm inside it, and then I lose the thread.

Learning how to go with the flow while still maintaining the core message is an art. When you learn to do that, you'll ensure you don't nibble your way lost.

Additionally, I find that often when someone is the founder of a brand, it can be delicate stuff to hand the representation of that brand to new people in the organization. Sometimes when you give your team a story to tell, it can go off the rails when they add their own spin to it. This leaves most leaders I know either frustrated, fearful, or possessive. They adopt an attitude of "Well, I guess I'll just have to do it myself" when it comes to sharing the company story.

When you understand where to bring personality into the structure of a story, though, multiple storytellers can share your brand story and smaller stories. Using a basic structure, each person in your organization can deliver the same story with their own flow and even adapt it to the audience in front of them. This gives everyone an authentic voice in telling the story without changing the facts.

It's not just team members who can lose the integrity of the story. If you have told a story so many times that you're months, even years, away from the original, it may be that you, too, have let it morph into something new. I'm often surprised by the choice line or excellent talking point I've left out of a workshop when I go back to the first draft. That's good stuff in there! How did I lose it?

And then there's the reality of what happens when you interact with the public and invite them into the story. So much discovery happens in that interaction. Often you can learn valuable things about your story by the response you get, and it's a good idea to incorporate those learnings into your narrative. However, it's important to know the difference between windows that can open and walls that can't be moved.

As a professional storyteller at Disney World, the number of times a guest said something in response to our script that was so funny and fresh we immediately stole it and made it part of the act are way too many to count. On occasion, the script would get so bogged down that we'd ask ourselves, "What parts did we add that are now slowing down the story line?" At that point, we'd revisit the original script, evaluate what we added, and make decisions about new bits that were funny and worth keeping, helped moved the story forward, or needed to go. When you start with a clear structure, you can revisit that structure to see if the flow and facts remain intact.

The pace and flow must also change to suit the audience. Let's say you want to use one piece of content—a story about how you innovated a system for your client—for a blog post. That's about five hundred to nine hundred words. The article may have photos and headers to break up the text. To promote that blog post, you want to share it on Instagram, Twitter, Facebook, and LinkedIn. But each of those platforms has a different style—visual, short and quippy, friendly, or professional. You'll need to adapt to each of those styles while maintaining the core message.

What if someone then reads your blog and decides to interview you on a podcast? Now you need to tell the story for an audio-only audience. Next you're invited to a networking group to share the three ways you innovated your client's system. That means you're going to do a live presentation with a PowerPoint.

Same message, different styles. You can use the tools in this chapter to find the foundational flow of your story and adapt it for each iteration.

Three-Act Structure

There are rules to story structure, but the flow can be adapted to the teller and the audience. Great storytellers know how to adapt a story to their unique voice and the present audience. But before we break a rule to our advantage, we need to know the rule.

The flow of your story follows the basic pattern of a three-act structure. In this chapter, we look at that three-act rule, how different styles use that structure, and, more importantly, how you can use it to create a framework to hang your story on.

We'll start with the story diagram. This is something you probably learned in high school English that you put behind you with that freshman essay on *Ethan Frome*. The classic flow of a story takes the shape of a triangle. The exposition is the starting point and considered act 1. Then the story makes the trek to the middle of the triangle with climbing action in act 2, driving to the climactic scene, the tip of the triangle. Then in act 3, there's a sharp decline, which signals the end and the falling action, or denouement.

What we often do when we're telling our stories, especially when we get nervous, is hang out in the exposition. Just as in the "Yes, Let's!" game, we're afraid to get to the action, so we turn the story into this. We babble on about place and time and explain what was happening before anything happened. Then we're forced to cram the action into a single moment, and we use the falling action to explain what we really meant. Deadly.

I can hear the sputtering now. You might be thinking, "But I need to set up the story! Everyone needs to know the company started in our garage and that the founders blah, blah, blah." Yes, I've relied on the excuse of "setup" many times—mostly when I wasn't sure where to start. The bottom line is, you don't need a setup. You need a story loop—a hook that opens a window into your world. That's act 1.

Let's go back to Oprah's speech at the Golden Globes and see where she opens that story loop that draws us in. It starts with, "In 1964, I was a little girl, sitting on the linoleum floor of my mother's house in Milwaukee, watching Anne Bancroft present the Oscar for best actor at the 36th Academy Awards." Oprah gives us the exposition—act 1—in a neat sentence. One sentence! She sets it up using just three facts: 1964, linoleum, watching. If you watch the video, you might even argue she opens the loop with a raised finger and the words "In 1964." That's all the exposition she needed to set up the story.

Continuing the three-act structure, we find the rising action of act 2 with this line: "She opened the envelope and said five words that literally made history: 'The winner is Sidney Poitier...'" And then the climax and denouement of act 3 happen here: "And it is not lost on me that at this moment, there are some little girls watching as I become the first black woman to be given this same award."

Once Oprah opens the story loop in act 1, she drives the tension through the rising action and reaches the climactic moment, when the main character has a realization that leads to a resolution. It's a masterful use of the tools that we're going to take out of the tool box in this section.

I'm convinced every great story operates in three acts—even Shakespeare's five-act dramas. You can see the beginning (Romeo sees Juliet at a party), the middle (they make a plan to be together), and the end (the plan ends in disaster with both of them dead). Sorry, I should have mentioned "spoiler alert."

You can find this flow in the classics, as well as in a classic tweet. Stephen King is a great one to follow on Twitter, where he delivers compact little stories in under 280 characters, as in this example: "I didn't use to watch THE PRICE IS RIGHT, but then I turned 70 and discovered it's the law."[7] The beginning is the setup, the middle is the action, and the end is the realization. Act 1, act 2, act 3—all in one little sentence. Perfect storytelling from the master.

When you see every story in the three-act structure, you can accordion a story, in and out, with details. For example, Stephen King could take this tweet and write a short paragraph for Facebook. Or he could expand it by adding more to each act and create an essay. I'd read that essay in *The New Yorker*, wouldn't you?

Don't Tell a Joke

I enjoy Jerry Seinfeld's *Comedians in Cars Getting Coffee* show, where he sits with other comics and dissects the nature of good comedy. The opening of the show is a joke itself—he sets us up by describing in detail the car he's chosen for his next guest—and then he offers the punch: "This is the perfect car for my coffee with Martin Short." If you're like me and let the episodes run one into the next, you find out the guest when he announces the name. All through the setup, you're waiting for the punch, trying to figure out who this car is like. And then bam! He hits you with it.

I love that Jerry uses the joke structure to open the show, but he's not necessarily trying to be funny. He uses the structure without really expecting the audience to laugh. Rather, it's a way to engage his audience. Think about a joke structure as a way to engage your audience. The setup and surprise offer a very pleasing experience—but a joke not everyone finds funny is not.

So let's take a moment and talk about opening speeches with a joke. Many people believe they need to open with a joke. The first question to ask is: Are you funny? Are you a naturally funny person? Do you say normal things and people laugh? If that happens, then you might be naturally funny. If being funny is a part of who you are, then it's a fine thing to use humor in your public speaking. If you tell jokes all the time and that's part of your personality, okay, maybe a joke at the beginning of a speech would work.

But let's think about this. When you're giving a speech, it's usually to a group of people who don't know you, and a joke can be like a glass of cold water thrown in the face of your audience. Some people will find it funny, some people will find it uncomfortable, and some people won't find it funny. Do you want to do that to your audience? I'll be honest. I don't want you to do that to your audience.

"But I need to get them going!" you might be saying. "I need to get them on my side!"

Yes, I've heard this before. Here's what you should do: open a story loop, and that will do it.

Here's an example of what I mean. I once worked with a beautiful and quiet young woman who leads workshops on creative practices. She's British and, to me, elegant and reserved. She often collaborated with American creative directors—you know the type I'm talking about: bowling shirts and goatees, riding skateboards through office halls. These guys kept telling her she needed to punch up the opening of her workshops to avoid losing her listeners. She should tell a joke, they thought.

So she crafted a joke that was passable. She could tell it and get a titter—which was really an attempt by the audience to placate her. In the South we'd say, "Bless her heart."

The thing is, telling a joke wasn't her. It was so apart from her personality that it didn't set up the rest of her talk. It wasn't anything like who she was going to be for the next hour, four hours, or three days as she and her clients worked together.

I asked her what had sparked her interest in creative practice, and she described her passion for the work of helping others use their creativity. She told me a beautiful story about how as a child, she could see the moon out the window of her home in Britain. She imagined her grandparents in India seeing the same moon. She described how she could see them in her mind's eye, just by looking at the moon. She built a bridge to them with her imagination, and then she grew up wanting to understand how the imagination works.

That story is interesting, compelling, and visual. It's much more engaging than a joke some guy wants you to tell. We crafted her opening to share that image and to ask her audience what sparked *their* imagination as a child.

If you think you need to tell a joke to get your audience to connect with you, I hope you'll find in the following tools some other options. Connecting with your audience through story creates a pathway to all sorts of opportunities. It's also possible the story might end up being funny.

The real question you need to answer is where you need your audience to be at the end of act 1. Do you need them energized? Unified? What are you trying to evoke? That will determine if you gather them close with a whisper and a secret or pump them up with music and a boisterous greeting. Figure out what your audience needs to go on the journey with you, and give that to them in the setup.

Joke Structure

If you are indeed funny, just know that a joke is a little story and should be crafted with the same intention. Three acts is the general arc of a story flow, but a joke is a setup and a punch. The setup is what happened before, and the punch is the surprising impact.

Let's go back to Jerry Seinfeld on this. Jerry attended David Byrne's Broadway show *American Utopia* and gave him some advice on how to close the show. I heard Byrne recount the story on a podcast,[8] and he said Seinfeld came right out and told him, "That one joke. You gotta fix it."

Byrne would close the show and set up the encore by saying, "The firemen don't want you to dance in the aisles, because the dancers in the aisles have an unfair advantage in the event of a fire." Seinfeld pointed out Byrne was jumping on top of his own joke—that the punch line of the joke was "unfair advantage," so that phrase should be at the end. Byrne updated the joke, fixing it to say, "The firemen don't want you to dance in the aisles, because in the event of a fire, the dancers in the aisles have an unfair advantage." Funny, right? Now the punch comes at the end.

The important thing to remember with a joke is that a joke takes the three-act structure and turns it into setup and punch. Applied to Byrnes's new version of the joke, the structure goes like this:

Act 1: Setup
The firemen don't want you to dance in the aisles,
Act 2: Action
because in the event of a fire, the dancers in the aisles
Act 3: Punch
have an unfair advantage.

The Rest of the Story

Another great methodology for story structure is "the rest of the story." This phrase was made famous by Paul Harvey, a radio personality. I listened to him on talk radio with my grandfather. We'd have our lunch and then we'd turn on Paul Harvey. I know this sounds like I was born in the 1930s and that during the war, my grandfather and I gathered around our wood-cased wireless for radio hour. But no. Harvey started in 1951 and was on the radio until 2009. I listened to him with my grandfather in the late 1980s, wearing gasket rings and acid-washed denim.

Harvey was a masterful storyteller on so many levels. His ability to color the story with details, drive up the tension, foreshadow the conclusion—all of it will keep you entranced. I always share one of Harvey's stories in my workshops because I want attendees to hear all those elements. But mostly I want to focus on this tool of "the rest of the story."

The broadcast always started with Harvey telling a story about something that wasn't going well. He didn't tell you who or what the subject of the story was. Rather, he described the desperate plight of the character, giving you clues along the way. And then, at the climactic moment, he'd go for the big reveal: "The young man's name? Abraham Lincoln." "The former loser and dropout? Albert Einstein." Then the denouement, which was a hearty laugh followed by his famous phrase: "And now you know...the *rest* of the story."

Everyone loves a reveal, and Harvey was the master. The key to "the rest of the story" is that we, the audience, are engaged in the story. We're not just waiting to hear the answer. If that were true, the minute we found out the answer, we'd be outta there. To use "the rest of the story" effectively, the story itself must be as engaging as the reveal. We want to be in that story, and the reveal is the cherry on top.

Another great example of the use of "the rest of the story" is found in Stephen King's book *On Writing*. In it, he offers his best advice for writers, which is bound to be pretty good advice, considering the source. Well worth the read.

King offers his advice by telling his life story—moments like when he discovered he wanted to be a writer, the many rejections he received, how he got up before dawn and wrote for hours before going to work. That story in itself is compelling, and then you get to the climactic moment of the book. Not many how-to books have a climax, but his is so well crafted that it does. It's at this climactic moment that he tells you "the rest of the story"—that all along, he was desperately addicted to alcohol.

It's a stunning shock, even if you know that's his history. You're so invested in the journey of his writing story that when he tells you "the rest of the story," you feel as though you should reread the whole thing through that lens. Not only does King give you writing advice in the book, but he opens a story loop you can't and don't want to get out of. He tells you how to write, he shows you how to write, and he gives you the experience of how he did it, all at the same time. He puts you in his story.

No matter what style you use to tell your stories, no matter what audience is listening to your story, the three-act structure gives you a flow that won't let you down. Open a loop and invite them in; drive up the tension through action; wrap up with a realization that satisfies and closes that loop. This creates the aha moment.

Working the Three Acts

Take the three-act structure of a story and see how it fits into the flow of your go-to story. Then experiment with moving things around. For example, I find that it helps when I move the climactic moment in my stories around. I might discover a new pace or a better moment to engage the audience.

Changing the flow usually comes down to audience and what meets the need of the moment. When I tell the "Feliz Navidad, Mickey" story to a group of marketers, writers, or communication pros, act 3 is all about teaching them to flip the script for maximum impact, just as I told it in chapter 2 of this book. That's the story they need to hear.

But when I tell that same story to entrepreneurs, executive directors, or human resource groups, I bring in the element of my personal life and add in the "rest of the story." I end act 2 by saying, "We saved Christmas. And I saved my job." Act 3 goes on to say, "You see, I didn't have a job once this holiday show closed. I was living at my parents' house with my autistic son, and I was on the brink of divorce. I needed that win. I couldn't afford a mediocre show. So I flipped the script, and learning how to do that changed the way I approach my work." This act 3 becomes a motivational speech, a "you can do this too" about being in a hard place and helping them figure out how to tell their story and take risks too.

Finding the flow of your story will be the same. It's always going to be the one that makes the most impact with the audience you're addressing at the moment. It's about discovering the flow that fits your pacing the best. I've used stories that worked fine, but when I moved one line forward in the story arc, it got a much better response—a gasp, a realization, or a nod from the audience that helps me discover the better flow for the story and where to place the climax.

I know it's scary to be up in front of an audience. For that reason, I don't consider it "practicing material" when I add something new or tweak it based on audience response. Though that's a tried-and-true exercise for stand-up comics, I am there to add value to my audience as a speaker. Switching things up and trying something new is more like an exchange. I have valuable information to share. They also provide valuable input, and as they respond, I learn how to improve the presentation.

Once Upon a Time

Stanislavski said acting is reacting. Stephen King said writing is rewriting. When we first offer up our story, it's raw. Sometimes it pours out of us. Sometimes it's a jumbled mess. We need to check for simplicity throughout the crafting process—because remember, we can nibble our way lost in our storytelling. If you have a story you've been telling about your organization for years, it's easy to add padding to it each time. You can forget that one thing that made it really pop. You need a simple way to reconnect and refresh your thinking.

The fourth item on Emma Coats's infamous list of Pixar's twenty-two rules of storytelling[9] is my go-to for getting to the simplest version of a story. The rule is: "Once upon a time there was _____. Every day, _____. One day _____. Because of that, _____. Until finally, _____."

For example: "Once upon a time there was an animation studio called Pixar. Every day, they created 3-D animated movies. One day, one of their artists, Emma Coats, tweeted twenty-two of their best practices for telling a story. Because of that, I discovered a simple way to check the crafting of my stories. Until finally, I was able to share that trick with you in this book."

The first question I get from students when I introduce this exercise is, "Do I have to tell my story this way?" No, of course not. This isn't a final draft—though I have had some clients use it to such great effect that they kept it for a pitch and it led to successful outcomes. Since we're always under pressure to be able to deliver our elevator speech, this exercise is a great way to find the bones of your pitch. It helps you see the skeleton that you can then dress up with muscle, tissue, flesh, and clothes.

Sometimes I get resistance on this exercise because it feels too simple and too childish. But simple is good. Childlike is good. This approach allows you to see the framework of your story. Here is how it looks when applied to our Oprah and "Feliz Navidad, Mickey" stories:

> Once upon a time there was a little girl sitting on the linoleum floor of her mother's house. Every day, she came home from school and watched TV by herself. One day, she saw a black man in a white tie receive a big award. Because of that, she realized she could be something more than a housekeeper like her mother. Until finally, she became the most powerful woman in all the world.

> Once upon a time there was an actor at Disney World. Every day, she went into the Mexico pavilion and told a holiday story. One day, she asked Mickey Mouse if he could wave to the kids in her audience. Because of that, she created a beautiful, magical holiday moment. Until finally, she had the confidence to flip the script in any situation.

This exercise boils your story down to its essence. You can use it to find the climactic moment and then condense the exposition of act 1. Work your story through the "Once Upon a Time" framework and see what you discover.

The good news about the tools of the storytelling trade is that you can use the tool that works for you and your specific audience and moment. You don't have to use all the tools every time. You can pick and choose the ones that work for you and for your audience. You can give the tools to your team, too, and each team member can then tell the same story, true to the brand but in their own genuine, authentic way. You can maintain brand integrity and tell your larger brand story through individual examples and stories. This way, you'll avoid sending brand robots in front of your audience to spout meaningless core values that don't connect.

With the tools in this chapter, you can find the flow of your story. You can begin to see the three-act structure. You can create a setup and punch. You can tell the rest of the story or a "once upon a time" fable. But even with all that, the emperor has no clothes—they are just naked stories. Time for some dress-up. In the next chapter, we'll take the hardest and most important rule for storytelling and make it work for you.

Takeaways:

✓ It's easy to nibble your way lost with your story. Be careful how many new parts you add in over time.

✓ Every story has a three-act structure—exposition, climbing action to climax, and resolution.

✓ When you see every story in the three-act structure, you can accordion a story, in and out, with details.

✓ Don't tell a joke—really, you don't need one. Instead, open a story loop.

✓ Consider telling "the rest of the story."

✓ Find the bones of your pitch by using the "Once Upon a Time" tool.

Chapter 6

Show, Don't Tell

Friends with the Fairy Godmother

For several years, I was "friends" with the Fairy Godmother. This is how we at Walt Disney World referred to the iconic roles we played. We didn't say, "I'm the Fairy Godmother," nor did we say, "I play the Fairy Godmother." For many—children and adults alike—these characters are real and live at Disney. That is to say, they fully inhabit the world they belong to, and that world happens to be inside a Disney theme park. They bring to life the imaginary reality of the park.

I'm sure you get what I mean. There is only one Tinkerbell that speeds across the night sky from the castle during the fireworks. There is only one Mickey Mouse, and he has many duties, from hosting parades to greeting guests to singing in shows. A roster of entertainers wear the mask, but there is only one Mickey. In the same way, there is only one Fairy Godmother—and a group of women, mostly in their mid-forties and up, who support her as "friends."

I became part of this coterie of women when I was a full-time improvisational storyteller at Epcot. Several times a year, I was invited to cover for actors who worked in other parks and went on vacation. My favorite cover was backing up those who were friends of the Fairy Godmother during her appearance in the castle restaurant. One fall, a friend of mine broke her ankle and she was off her feet for about six weeks. I stepped into her shoes at Cinderella's Royal Table during much of that time. The restaurant hosted a little show in which the Fairy Godmother and two mice, Suzy and Perla, would sing and dance to "Bibbidi-Bobbidi-Boo." There were celebrations and birthday songs and closing your eyes and making a wish. It was pure joy.

On my days off, I would do normal things, like grocery shopping and after-school pickup. When I was out and about, I got the distinct feel that small children were looking at me. They'd give me sidelong glances and giggle. They'd reach their small hands out from grocery carts to grab at me. Once, a neighbor's child bolted across the street while I emptied the trunk of my car. "She never does that!" her mother said, running after her. By the time mom picked her up, I had bent down and said, "I know, but please promise me you'll never run into a street again."

I checked with my group of friends, and yes, we all agreed this was normal. We also noticed it didn't stop once you weren't on call in the castle or in a parade. Years later, on an airplane from New York to Cairo, a grandmother traveling alone with a baby walked the aisle of the plane until she locked eyes with me. She didn't speak English, and I didn't speak Arabic, but I could tell she needed help. When I stood up, she put the infant in my arms and went to the lavatory. I rocked the baby, singing in her ear until grandma came back and settled in her seat, the infant back in her arms.

Embodying a story does that—especially a magical story about someone who makes dreams come true. I don't mean there's actual magic to it, but spending my nights gazing into children's eyes and telling them about the power of their dreams has a lingering effect. We become used to interacting with people through a story, so we keep doing it—whether in stores, in parking lots, or on planes.

Embodying a story is part of the most important rule of storytelling: "Show, Don't Tell." When I led those Brazilian teenagers through Disney Traditions, I spent the morning telling them about making the magic. But when I showed it to them, that's when they revealed their deep connection to the story. If you want to tell a story that moves people, you must use this hardest and most important rule in storytelling.

It's the only way to tell a story, actually, and it sounds deceptively simple but will challenge you the most. If you feel the emotion of the moment when telling a story, then it worked.

Let's say you write a simple sentence to describe your company on your website. You've gone through all the exercises and come up with a statement. Then your inner dialogue goes something like this: "Well, you know there were more people involved in founding the company. Remember Judy was part of it? She'll be upset if we don't mention her, even though she's moved on. And I remember the day we started the company in the garage—the air was kind of hot, so they probably need to know that. And of course, the reason it was important was that as a kid, I used to play in my garage when it got rainy, so I need to explain that too."

No one needs your explanation. They need a story, and a story is a picture your audience can see themselves in.

Paint a Picture

How do I know this works? Well, let's consider. What kind of floor did Oprah sit on? Yes, that's right. Linoleum. You'll never forget it because she painted that picture.

You can see it, can't you? You can even feel the linoleum, cool on the small girl's bare legs, because you know a little girl in 1964 wasn't wearing leggings. Little girls wore dresses. Do you see her Mary Jane shoes? I do. I imagine those folded-over white socks with a bit of lace that I wore on Sundays in 1972. Maybe you've seen photos of little Oprah in overalls with plastic clips in her pigtails and that is the little girl you see sitting on her folded knees on the floor in from of the TV.

She doesn't even say the word *television* in that part of her speech. She doesn't mention it was a black-and-white TV with rabbit ears, but you know it was. I see it on its spindly legs, its built-in square wood box with slightly rounded screen. Two large dials that *clunk, clunk, clunk* when you turn them. The two long, metal fingers of the antenna coming out the back. What does it look like to you? She didn't tell you it was a black-and-white TV. Rather, she *showed* you by saying just a few words: *1964, linoleum,* and *Oscars.* She showed you an image, and you painted the detailed picture of the rest. Did you see that magic trick? Your brain engaged, and you painted the rest of the picture.

What kind of hat did Mickey wear in my "Feliz Navidad, Mickey" story? When I ask this question in my workshops, I get many detailed descriptions of Mickey's holiday hat. Some people say it was a top hat with a sprig of holly in the band. Others know it was a Santa hat. Still others are positive it was a red and green knit cap with a fluffy ball on the top. The truth is, I don't even know. I've seen Mickey wear each of those holiday hats, and because every group has offered their suggestions with utter certainty, I no longer remember which hat he wore at the time. I can see the picture of him in my mind's eye wearing each of them.

When telling the "Feliz Navidad, Mickey" story, I take great pains to just say "holiday hat." If I told you exactly what Mickey Mouse wore, the specific details would have put you to sleep. When telling a story, you must leave room for the audience to paint themselves into the story.

This is a finer execution of the "Specific so we care" rule. You need rich detail, but not too much. You want to show the audience just enough detail to allow them to paint a picture in their imagination. This is key to the bonding process between you and your audience as you tell a story.

With "Show, Don't Tell," you again open a window into the story and your audience climbs right in. When you aren't telling them what to think, their mind activates and *they* start to think. They make the story their own.

This is good news if you're the one crafting the communication. You want your story to become the audience's story. But it's not very good news if you're a marketing person pitching the CEO, CFO, or board. Sometimes leaders worry about not spelling it out for the audience. Invariably, they'll say, "You need to tell them we served over 143,000 students in five counties. You need to tell them the data." I once had an executive director look over my shoulder at a presentation and say, "Take out all those photos and put in numbers on a plain background. No one cares about faces. They care about numbers."

Heavy sigh. It's actually the exact opposite. Your audience cares about faces first. Then they're interested in the numbers. Sometimes you can't convince your boss or your client that story will be the thing to woo your audience. Sometimes you need to take out the faces of children and put in the giant number because that's what that CEO needs.

Mostly, this is fear. It's scary when you open a window and allow someone else's imagination to engage. They'll add their story to yours. They'll abscond with your story and make it their own. They'll decide what hat your main character was wearing. It feels risky—and, in fact, it *is* risky. With "Show, Don't Tell," you can't control the response. When you tell someone, "Here are our impact numbers, and you need to give us this amount to solve your problems," you feel like you're in control. That's also an illusion. You may or may not be able to get someone to do what you tell them to do. If, however, you show them your mother's house and who you were as a little girl, they'll never forget the linoleum floor and they'll be bonded to you forever.

The good news is, you can weave data into your stories to please your client, boss, or prospect. To do that, though, you must be bold and learn to paint a picture. Trust that your audience will receive your message through a story. Trust that they'll connect with it and make it their own. Trust that your story will resonate on a deeper level than any figure or explanation. You've seen people in an art gallery gaze at a painting, taking it in, right? That's what you're going for with your audience. You're hoping they take it in and that it unleashes their imaginations and they begin to dream more vibrantly.

You can even paint a picture with your data. You can have both faces and numbers. For example, TED talks must match TED's mission of "ideas worth spreading," and speakers are given only eighteen minutes to share their big idea. Often they use metaphor and parable to maximize their time and paint a compelling picture. This is supported by TED founder Chris Anderson, who reminds speakers in his book, "If you're going to tell a story, make sure you know *why* you're telling it, and try to edit out all the details that are not needed to make your point, while still leaving enough in for people to vividly imagine what happened."[10] The power of inviting an audience to vividly imagine what happened, combined with your big idea or your data, makes for compelling storytelling.

Turn Numbers into Images

What do you do when you need to share important data, then? When you have room to tell a story and then show the data, do so. When you don't have time, try to turn numbers into images. Metaphors and parables are word pictures. They take ideas and turn them into pictures.

One of the word pictures that OCA found effective several years back happened because of the new autism diagnosis numbers released by the Centers for Disease Control in 2014. Silvia, the executive director, said to me, "It's now one in fifty-nine.

One in fifty-nine! These numbers are huge." She was convinced that if we just told that number to people, they'd realize how significantly autism impacted our communities.

I appreciated her passion, but I knew telling people that number would not alert them to the need. It would mean nothing to any listener. It meant nothing to me, and I was the "one" in that "one in fifty-nine" statistic! The difference between one in two hundred, one in fifty-nine, and one in sixty-five means... what? My brain doesn't receive this information as being important to survive or thrive, even though—again—I'm the one in fifty-nine.

The reason? I can't see the number.

Sylvia challenged me to come up with a meaningful way for her to use that number in a grant application, so I left the campus and drove home. As I went through the automatic gate of my suburban community, I started counting houses. I counted about twenty-three to a block, so two blocks equals forty-six. Midway through the third block, I hit fifty-nine.

Do you know what this means? Every three blocks, there's a kid with autism. Every three blocks, there's a family overwhelmed by therapy and aftercare bills. Every three blocks, someone is wondering about their child's future.

Now I get what that number means, because I can see it. It means there are other parents like me and other kids like Henry living just two-and-a-half blocks from my house.

When Silvia uses this metaphor now—with updated numbers, as autism's prevalence has only increased in the years since—along with stories of the individuals OCA serves, it gets a good response. People tell her that on their drive home, they found it impossible not notice the third block on their street and to imagine the families in their neighborhoods who might be overwhelmed by autism.

What numbers are you trying to communicate to your audience? What data do you need to get out there? Is there a word picture you can use? Look inside your company's context for symbols and images—kids on a playground, the fresh fruit section of the supermarket, a coffee shop or church on every block. What ordinary circumstances can you use to paint that picture? Then play with images outside your scope—cars on the Autobahn, birch trees in a forest, chickens in a coop.

Take one of your data points and come up with three word pictures like this. You may or may not end up using any of them. The goal of this exercise is to train your brain to look for the pictures that tell the story of your data. Don't worry if a metaphor doesn't hit or isn't perfect. Get yourself thinking in pictures. When you find the right metaphor, you'll be ready.

The Five Senses

Another important tool in "Show, Don't Tell" is using the five senses. This comes straight from the actor's toolkit. For an actor to bring a scene to life, they must imagine it fully, and that requires the five senses.

That might sound like a bunch of gobbledygook, so let me put it to you plainly. A good liar believes they've been where they said they were, even when they weren't. To make a lie believable, the teller must engage their five senses and "remember" an event that didn't happen. Have you met that person at work—the one who always has a tall tale? You know they're lying, but how do you know? Because they're telling you *about* an event, not reliving it.

I am sure Robert DeNiro does five-senses work. So do Meryl Streep and Viola Davis. You can see it in the performances, from Kristen Bell to Denzel. In your mind, you know that when an actor enters a scene, they've entered it from their trailer. They had to pass the craft services food table and stop by the wardrobe head, who checked their clothes. Then they stepped onto the set, where lights refocused, microphones got set, and a makeup artist patted powder on their face to avoid shine. Then the director said, "Action."

None of those things happened to the character they play in their scene. The actor must shed those sensory experiences and pretend they've had, instead, the sensory realities of the character. If they don't do that, we won't believe their entrance when we watch. Just like that one guy at work with the tall tale, we'll know they're lying.

In my workshops, I like to show a clip from the first Harry Potter movie, *Harry Potter and the Sorcerer's Stone*. It's Professor Snape's first appearance—one of my favorite movie entrances of all time. The door bangs open and in he flies, black robes waving like a flag behind him. As he marches to the front of the room, he says, "There will be no foolish wand waving or silly incantations in this class."

What was Snape doing moments before he entered the class where Harry Potter would be his student? It was a class he'd entered each year at the start of term. What would be different this year? Snape must have thought about what he needed to do to fulfill his mission to Lily Potter and Albus Dumbledore. He must have remembered the bullying he'd endured by Harry's father. He must have seen Lily Potter's eyes in his mind. Snape breathed deeply and opened the door.

Now, contrast that with Alan Rickman, the actor who played Snape. What was he doing in those moments prior to his entrance into the scene as Snape? Getting his wig fixed. Having his robe set so it would float behind him. Having a chat with the director about the scene. How many times did Rickman come through that door and shoot the scene? Five, ten, maybe twenty times. How many times did Snape come through that door? Once.

For Rickman to have made you and me believe he was really in that classroom rather than on a set, he had to imagine with all five senses the physical surroundings of the scene and the character's experience coming into the room. He also had to release the sensory experiences he had while coming from the trailer and imagine the sensory experiences of the character. In Rickman's case, he had to imagine a childhood history that included Harry Potter's mother; an ongoing relationship with his mentor, Albus Dumbledore; and being humiliated in school by Harry's father. That's why that entrance is so powerful. The flying robes and straight wig help—but without the sensory experiences he conjured and carried inside himself, we just wouldn't believe him.

You can bring your stories to life by evoking the five senses of your audience too. You don't need to become an actor and learn how to relive an event, and you don't have to fully imagine an experience one of your colleagues had so you can use their story. You just need to add details of your own. How do I know it works? Tell me again: What kind of floor was Oprah sitting on? Right again. Linoleum. You can feel it under your bare feet. That's sensory detail.

Go back to your story and ask yourself: What does it sound like? Smell like? Look like? Taste like? Feel like? What colors do you see? What textures do you feel? What sounds surround you? What scents are in the air? What senses are affected up close? What senses are in the periphery?

The benefit of exploring the full sensory experience is that you, like an actor in a scene, have imagined the entire story. You've seen it and felt it. Now you can create ways for your audience to climb right into the experience with you.

Fond Memory

Here's another exercise we do in our workshops. We break into pairs and tell each other about a vacation. We take five minutes for this, but the catch is that we don't tell stories of that vacation. We just describe the place. That's the objective of the exercise: a full sensory description. McDonald's, Nags Head, Girl Scout Jamboree, Vacation Bible School, Daytona Beach—we've heard descriptions of all of these, and more.

Ask a co-worker to do this exercise with you. You can use a vacation from your childhood or one you took a few years ago. Remember to focus on describing the location. You aren't sharing a story from the vacation or trying to evoke a feeling. After you've shared, debrief and answer these questions using one-word descriptors or short phrases:

- What sounds did you hear?
- What colors did you see?

- What smells did you relive?
- What did you touch with your hands? Your feet?
- What temperatures did you feel?
- What flavors did you taste?

The reason I ask you to answer these questions with one-word descriptors or short phrases is because it keeps you focused on the sensory details you heard. Take, for example, this story from someone who didn't think they had much of a story to share: "Well, my experience wasn't really a vacation. My family didn't really get a vacation, so we went camping out in our back-yard with a tent, and there were fireflies, and we caught them in mason jars and pulled weeds with our hands and put them in the jars, and all three of us kids danced around the backyard with our jars of lightning bugs."

Okay, let's debrief that story. You heard: *weeds snap, jar lid click, parents' voices, laughs, whispers*. You saw: *night sky, blue, stars, fireflies, flashes of light*. You felt: *vinyl, cloth, tent, grass on feet*. You smelled: *night air, grass, dirt*. You tasted: *juice, peanut butter, grass, popcorn*.

These exercises give you a 3-D view of your story. Now you've got a palette of sensory details to choose from and can add dabs of them as you go. Remember that Oprah didn't over-paint her story with sensory images. She gave you just enough to put you in the room with her little-girl self.

Now take a look at the "Once Upon A Time" version of your story and reread it with the sensory details in mind. Notice how the simple version becomes richer and more lay-ered. By sprinkling in a few details, you open that window for your listeners to climb right in and paint the story using their imagination.

You can pick and choose from your list of sensory descriptions and sprinkle them into your story. I considered more sensory details in my story than I shared with you. In crafting the story, I made sure there were enough specifics for you to care, but not so many that you got bored. How did I choose which ones to keep? I focused on the audience's problem and how this story solved it. That helps me to fine-tune the sensory descriptions. I want them to have a "linoleum floor" moment and to be empowered by their own ability to imagine the black-and-white TV. When you give your audience room for their imaginations to paint the scene, they won't tune out.

Speaker's Point of View

An important consideration in crafting the right story for the right moment is not only your audience but who the speaker is. If you're the founder or CEO of an organization, most of the time it's you. But say you get bigger and add more people to your team. Other people might speak on behalf of your company, and this is when you need to consider their role and their personality. The introverted founder can tell just as good a story as the exuberant sales executive. Remember the leader who only wanted numbers and no faces? You can accommodate this approach and still use story. The CFO and the passionate volunteer have different perspectives on the company, and you can help them both tell stories.

I was working with the CEO of a food bank that serves eight counties in Florida. We were trying to find her best story. She was describing individuals who had benefitted from the program—a man getting a bag of rice, a child getting a Cutie clementine—and they were all completely appropriate, true, and typical. I asked who gathered these stories for her. Was she in the food bank daily, or did she hear them from some of her frontline workers?

"Oh, we serve fifteen different food banks in this county alone," she said. "I'm at a warehouse each day, overseeing distribution of several tons of food. These are stories from the people who work with our clients face to face."

"Ah ha!" I said. "Well, share something that happened in your day, then."

She went on to tell an incredible story about a truck that had been loaded with two tons of potatoes. The trucker was to deliver the potatoes to a large grocery store chain but missed his morning window and didn't get there until after ten that night. When he finally arrived, the manager of the store turned him away because they no longer needed the shipment. The truck driver had to get rid of the potatoes, though, so he could pick up his next load. The store manager put the driver in touch with the CEO, who told him to head to a rest stop on I-95, outside of Jacksonville. Then the CEO started calling volunteers with pickup trucks and SUVs. Staff members got U-Haul trucks from the main warehouse. All of them met at the rest stop and unloaded the potatoes into the twenty-eight trucks that showed up. Then the volunteers and staff drove to fifteen food banks across the county and unloaded.

Ding, ding, ding! We have a winner! While the story of a small child getting a clementine for the first time in a month is, of course, important, it's also a story we expect to hear from a food bank and will hear from any number of people associated with the organization. But this story was the CEO's own experience, not that of a volunteer or someone else on the front lines.

Additionally, the potato truck story did a few things for us, her audience. First, it showed impact. She didn't have to present a chart with data about how far the organization reached—a semitruck full of potatoes is an image. A Ford Explorer filled to the brim with potatoes is a picture. More than twenty SUVs and pickup trucks driving in different directions from a rest stop shows me the scope of the region it covers. Could she follow this story with a pie chart and numbers? Yes, and now those charts and graphs would make an even greater impact because, thanks to the story, we can see them in a more relatable way.

Second, this is a story the CEO could tell with passion because it happened to her. It happens to her all the time. When she shares this story and then hands a donor a brochure that describes the volunteer's encounter with a hungry child getting that tangerine, that story now has even more impact. She's shown us her story, and now we're in the story loop. We've painted ourselves into the picture, and we can see both stories and experience the impact of both.

The potato truck story is one I use to highlight how to get data into your stories. Invariably, someone on your board or in your leadership team will insist you show the chart: "Cut the story and show the data! People need to know how many people we served and how much money we spent on this and how much comes in from that grant and where the need is." So get out your three lists: universal, specific, and action. Put those next to the data. Is there a story that can show some of that data? The potato truck story reveals what the charts and graphs mean. Present the data, and then show its meaning with a story. Two tons of potatoes in a semitruck at a rest stop being unloaded by friends and neighbors into their SUVs is an image I won't soon forget—although I might forget that you distribute over thirty-one million pounds of food.

The Five Ws

Sometimes when you're in the weeds of a story, it can help to bring it back to the basics with the five Ws: Who, What, When, Where, Why, and How (the one non-W word). I use the Ws in a different order than your English grammar textbook and suggest instead a flow that helps you find the main character, the plot points, and what drives the character from one point to the next.

I start with Where, because that helps us get into the sensory specifics of the story first—just like we did with the vacation exercise. List all that goes with the Where of the story—the setting, the time, the place. Get specific. If it's a conference room, where is it located? What does it look like? How is decorated?

After Where, concentrate on Who. Who are the people in the story? Their roles? Their personalities? What motivates them? What do each of them want? What do they need? Beyond the main character, every character in a story must also have a want. If they don't want something, there's no story. People who *want* something are motivated to *do* something. You should spend some time coming up with a want for every character on your Who list.

Let's take one of the stories we've talked about already: the children's cancer research charity. What did the mom want? Healing for her son and a cure for cancer, of course. But dig deeper. What motivated her to start a whole organization dedicated to this research? I mean, that's a lot of work! Especially when you're caring for a child with an illness, not to mention any other children she may have, plus work, family life, and a home. What did she *really* want? Answers. She wanted answers.

Dig deep into the wants of the individuals involved in your story. To get out of bed and pursue something that seems unattainable—a meal, a job, a cure for cancer, an artistic expression, a change in the community—you must have a want that pushes you to take each step. If the want isn't strong enough, then we give up when the next step gets too hard. (Check my WW points tracker and my Fitbit if you're confused on this point. I keep track for a week or two, and then I think, why bother?)

Identifying the characters and their wants brings us to the When. When did something happen that made you or the people in your story dig in? When did a challenge arise that they had to meet? The characters in your story must have had a conflict they needed to overcome. What was it? That conflict created the inciting incident, and the inciting incident is the event that drives the entire story.

In the potato truck story, if the Who was the driver, the inciting incident would have been being turned away by the store manager. But since the Who was the CEO, the inciting incident was the phone call from the store manager.

When do you get to the inciting incident in your story, see if it comes too late into the narrative. When the inciting incident appears is key to the flow of your story. It's the event that drives the story. Remember when we talked about act 1 and exposition and how we tend to blather on during that time, just to make sure the setup is clear? The inciting incident solves that problem. It must come early on in the story. Don't wander in circles! Get to the action with the inciting incident. "In 1964, I was a little girl, sitting on the linoleum floor watching Anne Bancroft"—there's the inciting incident. Because Oprah was watching Anne Bancroft, the rest of the events in her life unfolded. Look at when it happens: third verb of the first sentence. Boom! We're on a ride.

The inciting incident flows into the What. These are your plot points, the action that happens as a result of the inciting incident.

So we've covered Where, Who, When, and What. These first four Ws bring you to the How. How did this impact those involved? Under this heading, list the outcome, the decision, or the resolution that came about from taking this ride along the plot points. This will help you find the climactic moment of your story.

This part of the exercise can help you find your conclusion, the ending to your story. Often when we tell a story in conversation, we trail off with the ending. You start to wind down and say, "Well, you know…," and then someone else in the conversation shares their own story or starts a new thread of conversation. If this were just a conversation, this would be fine. But when you tell a story for your brand or about your impact, you need to share your conclusion.

In telling my "Feliz Navidad, Mickey" story, I try to share a vivid visual representation of me as a storyteller to give seminar participants a chance to see me in action and give them confidence. However, that's not the conclusion to that story. The resolution needed to be an outcome that was about the audience, not me. That experience, for me, was about learning to flip the script to meet the moment. Why did I want to share it with you? So you could learn how to meet the moment of your own storytelling opportunities.

Which brings us to Why. This is your universal theme that floats over the whole story. Why does this story matter, and what is the meaning running through this story? What universal truth is here to which everyone can relate? To use the marketing lingo of many a creative director, what is the "so what"?

Back to Mickey. The reason I use the "Feliz Navidad, Mickey" story is because I was leading an eight-hour workshop and after lunch I got a question on this story technique that I wasn't prepared for. The question was, "Can you give us an example?" I thought for a minute, then launched into this story. As I was telling it, I could see they were captivated. I could see the red bus and the Mickey hat delighting them, but why were they so rapt? It's because of the Why. Why this story matters is that I was in a difficult situation and found a way out. Every single person in that room could relate to that, especially as it pertained to our workshop topic, which happened to be about pitching to donors using story. Each person in that room had been in front of another kind of room, asking for money, and bombed. They'd told a story that didn't work. I was sharing with them how I found a way to make a story work.

And there was a red bus with Mickey Mouse in it. Bonus!

This tool can help you find the universal truth in each story. It can also help you find the inciting incident and clear out the clutter around your story's plot points. To find the bones of your story, you can approach the use of this tool two ways. One is as a flow chart, with each of the Ws flowing down the page, connected by arrows: Where > Who > When > What > How > Why. Or you can use a series of bulleted lists. Whichever approach you use, I recommend keeping it all on one page so you can see the X-ray of the skeleton's form in one place.

The Greatest Talk Show Story Ever Told

For more than fifteen years, Jay Thomas appeared on David Letterman's Christmas program. Other annual segments included the throwing of a football to dislodge the Christmas meatball on top of the tree and Darlene Love closing out the show with "Christmas (Baby Please Come Home)." It made sense to include the song every year—it's a classic, and Darlene Love was spectacular. And the meatball challenge was different every year because you never knew which guest, or if the host himself, would actually knock the meatball off its perch. But the same guest telling the same story, year after year, in the same slot? Unheard of—except for the brilliance of this story and how it was told.

I'll recap the story for you—but better yet, search for it on YouTube. You won't regret watching it.

Jay Thomas was an actor and raconteur. In fact, in the later part of his career, he had a radio show where he recounted interesting stories and interviewed guests. Of all the Christmas appearances he did on Letterman's show, I like the early ones best, from the late 1990s. In those visits, he masterfully delivered on all the elements we've talked about so far.

The story goes that Thomas was a DJ in Cincinnati, Ohio, and often would do live promotions. He describes himself as "a hippie with a white man's afro" and his friend as "a long-haired dude." At one of these events, the draw was that Clayton Moore, the actor who played the Lone Ranger in the classic TV western, would be there to sign autographs.

Moore arrived in the expected blue jumpsuit with black mask and white hat, as he did whenever he had an appearance booked, and while Moore was with the crowd, Thomas and his buddy went behind a dumpster and got "herbed up." At the end of the event, the car that was to take Moore back to his motel didn't show, so Thomas and his buddy offered to drive him. They got into Thomas's beat-up Volvo and headed out.

On the drive, a businessman pulled out and backed into Thomas's car, smashing the front headlight and quickly driving away. Thomas and his buddy forgot Moore was in the back and took off after the other car.

When they finally caught up with him, they confronted the driver. "You smashed my car!" Thomas said. The man took one look at the Volvo and these guys and said, "No, I didn't." They knew he did, so they accused him again: "We're going to call the cops." The man replied, "Oh yeah? Well, who are they gonna believe—me or you two hippie freaks?" Out of the back of the Volvo came the Lone Ranger. "They'll believe me, citizen," Moore said. The man jumped back and said, "I didn't know it was you!"

It is the most perfectly satisfying story. So satisfying that I absolutely counted myself among the viewing audience members who tuned in every year just to hear it retold. I wanted to be pulled in again and to experience it with Jay and Dave every year.

So why did I, and many others, want to hear it over and over? What was so compelling about it? Let's look at the tools we've already unpacked from your toolkit.

First, structure and flow. The story has a three-act structure—a beginning, middle, and end. There's also an inciting incident that ropes us in, an ordinary event that this time includes the Lone Ranger.

The Ws are crystal clear. We know where they are, who they are, and what happens as the plot points follow—*boom, boom, boom*. The climax of the story is a perfectly timed How, with the statement from the antagonist: "Who they gonna believe—me or you two hippie freaks?" When that climactic moment hits, it's both expected and totally unexpected. We're certain the Lone Ranger is going to save the day. We just don't know how or in whose favor the rescue will go. The denouement—"I didn't know it was you!"—brings the story to a swift and satisfying close.

Now let's look at the story elements. Thomas takes us into the scene with complete "Show, Don't Tell." We're there through the gloriously painted specifics that bring it to life and make us care—the white man's afro, getting "herbed up," a car lot in Cincinnati, the banged-up Volvo, the blue suit, and the mask. Does he mention the white hat and silver badge? No, he doesn't, but we see it. He doesn't need to tell us every detail. Remember how it works. He invited us into the picture, and we painted it for ourselves.

Universal so we can relate? You bet. We may never have been an herbed-up 1970s DJ, hauling the Lone Ranger through Cincinnati in our beat-up Volvo, but each of us has experienced a moment when we felt unjustly attacked and hoped for a *deus ex machina* to descend and resolve the situation in our favor.

What's more, that universal theme trips our brains into survive-and-thrive mode. We're hooked because many of us have experienced being in a lousy job, and likely even slacking off. Then a situation arises that demands we stand up and survive. We're off, chasing the bad guy. When accused of our laziness, a god rises up from the back seat to declare our innocence. Survive and thrive.

"Show, Don't Tell" is the hardest rule to follow. It seems ambiguous. How do I know when I'm telling, not showing? It's also surprisingly easy to defend boring choices with a quick "Yeah, but I'm showing—see, I mentioned the color of the car here!" But you do know the difference between an interesting story, where everyone leans in, and a boring story, where everyone tunes out.

Here's the thing. Telling a good story is hard. When you're sweating it out in front of a blank page, you're not wrong. It's hard work. That's why there are so many tools in this chapter to help you tell your story and tell it well. These are tools you can play with, not rules to rigidly follow. Put one of these tools on your blank page, and voila! The page is no longer blank. Play around until you find your potato truck, your red bus, your Lone Ranger, or your linoleum floor. I promise it's in there.

Takeaways:

- ✓ "Show, Don't Tell" is the most important rule in storytelling. It's also the hardest.
- ✓ Show the audience just enough detail to allow them to paint a picture in their imagination.

✓ Your audience cares about faces first. Then they care about data.

✓ Turn ideas into pictures using metaphors.

✓ Use the five senses to bring a story to life.

✓ The "Five Ws" tool can bring your story back to basics when you find yourself in the weeds.

Part III
Deliver

Chapter 7

Master Your Delivery

Bear Country USA

On one of our cross-country trips from Idaho to Virginia, the three of us kids wanted to see wildlife. A driving trip through Bear Country USA seemed just the right solution. See the bears from your car! See the bears in their natural habitat! While it sounded very *Mutual of Omaha's Wild Kingdom*, one of their natural habitats was having a guy in the back of a pickup truck fling raw meat at them. I know this because somehow the path we took landed our sky blue K-car wagon right behind the pickup. As the bears raced past our flimsy doors, my mother screamed, "Herb! Don't hit one of them or they'll all rise up and kill us!"

Our gales of laughter continued through Wyoming and into Montana. As unlikely as it was that the bears would care about us even if we knocked one of them off, to this day my poor mother, now well into her eighties, endures ribbing about her warning: "Don't hit one of them or they'll all rise up and kill us!"

It's just as unlikely that the staff is going to rise up and kill you after a poor PowerPoint presentation. Or that the passengers of the elevator will attack you after your failed elevator pitch. Regardless, when a group of people looks expectantly at you, your mouth can go dry and your hands start to shake. Everything in your body screams, "I don't belong here!" The nervous energy builds until you find your limbs and vocal cords controlled by the energy of flight, fight, or freeze.

One way to master your delivery is to reframe the situation. Your goal for a presentation is not perfection or sales or applause. It's about connection. I know pitching to a conference room, or even to a client one-on-one, doesn't always feel like making a connection. It can feel more like standing on a cliff with angry bears prowling below, ready to devour you. I promise that if you flip this script, you'll experience greater success in your presentations.

Once again, your presentation of your story is not about *you* and how you're doing. It's about *them*, your audience. You can bring this delivery piece back to the Story Formula, just like everything else. By connecting your story's specific details with a universal theme and intention, you can learn to regulate and use your breath, your energy, your audience's energy, and your audience's expectations to take them where you want them to go. That's the work we'll do in this chapter, and it will transform how you present your content, both in person or on screen.

The bottom line is, your audience connects best with your genuine self through a natural delivery. You can have a beautifully crafted speech, but if you don't know how to deliver it, your message won't reach your audience. And believe it or not, you already have a natural, pleasing delivery. The good news is that it's easy to find and maintain—though it's not likely the same delivery you're using now. You're probably operating in a mode that's guided by your nerves and your image of what makes a good speaker. This is a deadly combination and usually creates more nervous energy, which gets you further from your authentic self. Your genuine presence and voice will be your greatest tool for getting your unique message across.

The same goes for crafting messages in email or on social media. Here, we're looking for our authentic voice to translate onto the page. Although this chapter focuses on in-person and live delivery scenarios, the same principles apply to developing your voice online and in print. The further we are from our authentic voice when we present, the further we'll be when we write.

If you're not sure what I'm talking about, watch any episode of *Judge Judy*, *The People's Court*, or any of the myriad "real" court shows. The minute the person standing before the judge opens their mouth to speak, they use words and a tone they've likely never used before: "Well, you see, your honor, the defendant traversed the street, congregating adjacent to my vehicle, and I reacted with intensity." What they probably said to their friend on the day it happened was, "That jerk walked right over to my car, so I screamed at him to get away."

The energy you want to have when you give a speech or deliver a presentation is almost the exact opposite of the nerves you experience when you get up in front of people. What I mean is, you need to be warm, relaxed, and engaged. Instead, your nerves give you short and shallow breath, tightness in your voice, and tension in your shoulders. Ugh. Flight, fight, or freeze is the default for your operating system, and when you get up in front of a group of people, your system registers it as a dangerous situation. They could all rise up and kill you!

The goal is for you to be in charge, not in the flight, fight, or freeze energy. Rather than experiencing your nerves, what you need is to be relaxed and energized, whether you're giving a TED talk or a department presentation, a Zoom webinar or a job interview.

To achieve a more peaceful state, people often try to conquer their nerves with relaxation techniques. But Zen energy alone isn't ideal. You must meet the audience at their energy level. You must bring some energy of your own too—some excitement for your product or service to the table.

Other people take the opposite path of pumping themselves up, trying to get into an optimal performance zone. Jumping up and down or pounding your chest can get you into a Tony Robbins sort of energetic state. This can result in too much energy, though, and you may overwhelm your audience.

Relaxed and energized is the perfect state for any presentation. When you're relaxed, you're calm and can evaluate the energy around you and adjust your content to meet the moment. You can capture the energy of the group and move them to the level of energy you want for them to participate in your goals. When you're *slightly* energized, you present an interesting new kind of energy to the group. They can feel you have something interesting to offer, something going on, and they want to be a part of it.

How do you replace flight, fight, or freeze with relaxed and energized? With some very simple techniques you can do in your car on the way to an event—or even in the moments before you walk through the door or face the camera. Time to open up the actor's toolkit. Many acting programs challenge students to do a twenty-minute warm-up before they take the stage. I'm sure twenty minutes is great for those performing a Shakespearean drama for several hours. For me, doing a twenty-minute warm-up for a twenty-five-minute show at a theme park—that's overkill. Also, I'm not a person that sits still well. On my daily meditation app, I can do about five minutes of the fifteen-minute meditation. If you have twenty minutes to prepare yourself, go for it. If you have thirty seconds, here's what you can do.

Shake-Outs

Stand up, with your arms at your side. Lift your right arm slightly from your body and give it a shake. Now let it back down. Feel the difference between your right arm and your left. Do you feel the tingling? It feels a little bit alive, a little more present while still relaxed, along your right side. That's relaxed and energized.

Now do the same thing with your left arm. Now your right foot. And your left foot. Your entire body is now in a state of relaxed and energized. This is the feeling you want when you speak.

In this state of relaxed and energized, notice your feet planted on the ground. Feel the floor beneath you. Feel the gravity and how much support it gives you. Notice you have total control over your feet and how solid they feel to the foundation of the earth beneath you.

Shake out your arms and legs again. Feel the light energy tingling through your arms and legs, like a little electrical circuit coursing up and down. You own that energy. You are in command of your body. Your body can't rise up and do something you don't know it's going to do. You're totally aware of the energy of your limbs, your fingers, your knees. Your hands will *not* flail in nervous energy. Your knees will *not* give out from fear. Your shoulders will *not* tense, awaiting assault. You own the space you occupy. You don't have to prove your right to be there. You've just defeated fight.

You can defeat flight and freeze through deep breathing. Nerves stop your breath in your chest, cutting off your breath and making it go shallow. The first step is to release the hold on your lower belly. I can guarantee you're trying to suck in your gut. Let it go. Put your hand on your belly button if you need help feeling your breath moving past your chest. Breathe in to a count of four, and breathe out to a count of four. Take the out breath to a count of five if you can.

Thirty seconds, easy. Sixty seconds, tops. You're relaxed and energized, no longer operating in fight, flight, or freeze. Being grounded and energized puts you in charge of your body. This is important because without control of your body, your nerves will attempt a coup. When you're aware that speaking activates the fight, flight, or freeze mechanism in your system, you can override it with this relaxed-and-energized exercise.

Move or Don't Move

Before you take the stage, you want to make a plan for how you'll move. I don't mean you should choreograph your movements or diagram when you'll raise your hand to make a point. Actors in the theater have a strong and simple rule: move or don't move.

This sounds idiotic, I'm sure. Of course you would either move or not move. But a theater stage is about five feet above the floor. When you get on a stage, everyone looks up at you. This can make you feel like you need to move. Your right leg starts to walk, but you think to yourself, "Wait, do I want to move now? Is now a good time?" But the leg has already started, so you take a sort of strange half-step. Your arm raises, and it feels like a significant gesture—because on the stage, five feet up, any movement is significant. You notice your arm moving, and you get nervous. Why is it doing that? So you half-raise your arm and then leave it hanging in midair.

These random half-movements happen all the time to speakers. The solution is simple: move or don't move.

In real life, when you're sitting at a table, you might brush a stray hair off your shoulder, fiddle with a pen, or scratch your nose while sitting across from other people, talking about Facebook metrics. No one notices. Everyone else at the table is doing the same thing—seeing a piece of fuzz on their shirt, flicking it off, picking up a pen, putting it down. On a stage, raised above the crowd and with everyone looking at you, any movement or gesture looks like you're trying to make a point. This is true on camera as well. Movement means something when it's captured by a lens. It looks significant. So decide in advance: move or don't move.

Not moving means letting your arms rest at your side. On stage, at a podium, or at the front of a room, your arms hanging by your side looks natural to your audience. In real life, your arms hanging by your side, not gesticulating, appears stiff. This seems counterintuitive, but if you're relaxed and energized, your arms resting at your sides is a very pleasing stance to an audience. It makes them relaxed and energized too.

If you want to take a step or move your arm, do so. Move. If you urgently think, "I'm supposed to move," and you feel your body trying to figure out if it should raise an arm, don't move. Those are your nerves trying gain control. Breathe. Then *you* choose: move or don't move.

Eye Contact

To create a connection with your audience, eye contact is the trajectory beam that draws individuals in. When you look someone in the eye, they know they've been seen. On the list of universal themes, self-actualization, or being seen and heard, is one of our deepest needs.

Eye contact can be uncomfortable in one-on-one settings, so I practice the Swedish method of *skol*. When I was a teenager, my dad was appointed the naval attaché to Sweden. He and my mother went through a year of protocol training to understand Swedish culture and customs. *Skol* is an important connecting ritual at formal Swedish dinner parties, and likely at more casual ones too. *Skol* is connection. It's a toast, like "cheers," but more formal—and yet also more warm than the dreaded best-man toast at a wedding here in the United States.

In Sweden, when a toast is given by the host or guest of honor, everyone at the table raises their glass. The glass is raised to about the level of your chin, and you look into the eyes of the person across from you. Your eyes meet, you both say *"Skol,"* and then you drink. You're not done yet, though. The connection is still there. After you drink, lower your glass to the front of your chin again, and look back into the eyes of the person you were *skol*-ing with. Now release. You'll *skol* with everyone else at the table. It's easy to get drunk at a Swedish dinner party.

I love this exercise because it's a warm and meaningful look into someone's eyes, and possibly a stranger's eyes. It's just about the amount of time we can stand to look directly into someone's eyes—about three seconds, drink, another three seconds. We do this in our classes with our iced tea and water bottles.

I recommend you ask some friends or colleagues at work to *skol* at least once. Get a feel for what it's like to hold someone's gaze for that amount of time. Then in a presentation or a pitch meeting, you'll be comfortable with a warm but short amount of meaningful eye contact.

Three-Camera Shoot

Do you remember the old adage to imagine your audience in their underwear to help your nerves? I can't imagine worse advice. Not only would you be facing down an audience that makes you nervous, now they're all in their drawers. I'm a fan of picking out individuals in a crowd and making them your friends, whether you know them or not. Seeing an audience as friendly, interested individuals is a much better way to tame nerves.

When you're in a room with tables, speaking to a large group—say, at a conference—use the three-camera method. If the event is being filmed, you'll probably see three cameras: one at the midway point in the room on the right side, one midway on the left side, and one all the way in the back, in the center of the room. Use these positions, whether there are cameras or not, to pick out a table or a person in those locations. If there are cameras, look at the people right in front of the camera setup. You're looking for eyes, not lenses. Then, throughout your talk, direct portions of it to your new friends in each of these three sections. This keeps your connection with people going, keeps your body movements fluid, and makes sure everyone in the room feels included through your eye contact.

If you are live in a room and the talk is being filmed, let the camera pick you up. Let it do the work of connection. Focus on your live audience, and use the placement of the cameras in the room as the points toward which you can move your face and your focus. You don't need to speak directly into the cameras.

In our virtual world, it's all about looking directly into the camera. But looking directly into the lens, unblinking, can make you come across like a late-night infomercial host, trying to convince viewers to purchase a revolutionary food chopper. On a movie set, when actors speak to a camera, often someone stands next to the lens, and they speak their lines to the person. They make eye contact with the person, not the lens.

If you're used to doing live talks, then you have a feel for the energy in the room. This can be difficult to translate online. When we try to connect with an audience on camera in the same way we connect with a live group, we can come at the camera with too much energy. The energy is different, so even if you're talking to multiple people or have an audience online, the better approach is a conversational manner. When you need to look into a camera, imagine a friend on the other side of that lens.

In a virtual session, be it a panel interview or a group meeting, you might have the same number of people you would have in a board room or meeting hall. I attended many webinars by famous speakers who went virtual during the pandemic. They were masterful at adjusting their arena energy to conversation-with-friends energy, even though they presenting the same material they'd usually present in a three-thousand-seat hall.

The bottom line is that choosing to see your audience as friends will help you focus any nervous energy into performance energy. It will create a warm and inviting atmosphere. Seeing a Zoom room or a ballroom full of an "audience" can make you feel alone and like the bears will all rise up and kill you. Even if you imagine them in their underwear, it's still a group that could be hostile and semi-clad. Make them your friends instead.

Make Friends

Making friends with individuals in your audience through eye contact may feel awkward at first, but I'll tell you a secret—they don't know you're doing it. Audience members do not think you are singling them out. They feel removed as viewers, even at a live event.

I can prove it to you. I was doing a show at Walt Disney World on Father's Day. We were out in Epcot's United Kingdom pavilion, and the street was full of people down to the crossroads, packed in to watch our comedy show. It was my job to pick an audience member for the role of Sir Lancelot in our fractured King Arthur story. I was looking for a fun dad. I scanned the crowd of baseball-capped dads and saw a really fun Drew Carey–type standing at the back of the audience. He had a crew cut and cute, nerdy glasses. Perfect! I looked him in the eyes, and for the first time in my then ten years of doing interactive comedy shows, the guy looked back at me. He gave me a wink and a very short shake of his head, "No."

Now, I've been rejected by audience members many times, but usually it happened when I walked toward them or when I put my hand on their shoulder and said, "Here he is, Sir Lancelot!" No one before, and no one since, has ever looked back at me when I made eye contact from a stage across a sea of audience members. Never. That's because this guy actually was Drew Carey.

Drew Carey was, at that time, very much an everyman character on his shows, *The Drew Carey Show* and *Whose Line Is It Anyway?* Even though he was so very popular, he melted into the crowd. No one in the audience knew it was him. I didn't recognize him at first, either. The only reason I realized it was him was because of his response to me. Only another performer would know I was looking directly at him. Every other audience member thinks I'm looking in their general direction.

Drew Carey watched the whole show that afternoon, at one point even coming up to the front row and sitting on the curb. No one noticed him.

Don't be afraid to look an audience member in the eye. Individuals in a crowd do not feel singled out. They don't notice what is going on with other individuals. They respond as a collective. Unless it's Drew Carey, they'll never know.

Play the Balcony

In larger arenas, conference halls, or theaters, you can't make eye contact with every person in attendance. You can, however, create eye contact with the crowd. In musical theater, we're taught to "play the balcony." That means lifting your face to the top level of the theater when singing a song. Performing to the first three rows right in front of you is tempting, because you can actually see those faces. If you do that, though, the middle sections of the orchestra, the mezzanine, and the balcony only see the top of your forehead. You cut off more than three quarters of your audience.

Raise your face and play the balcony in a larger space. Miraculously, this technique allows the people in front to feel included and the people in back to feel seen.

Natural Voice

The other key ingredient to your natural delivery is, of course, your voice. As an audience member, it makes me nervous when someone speaks in an unnatural voice. When they're trying to make a sale, trying to sound impressive, or even trying to sound pleasing, the effort usually restricts their natural voice. The key word there is *trying*. When you start from your relaxed, energized presence and your natural voice, you start from your zone of confidence.

That forced, false voice happens when the nerves take over and squeeze the air out of your body. Your voice pitches too high and gets strident. But when you try to sound smooth, your voice drops and registers too low. If you try to grab control, you end up sounding exactly that way—grabby and needy.

Your natural voice is the most pleasing voice. I know that seems wrong—you probably don't like your voice on recordings. You think it's not commanding enough. It sounds too nasally or too breathy. It's just weird sounding. Believe me, I know. I've heard my own voice in voiceovers I was paid to do and thought, "Is that what I sound like?" But your natural voice is the most genuine version of you. As vulnerable as it seems, speaking in your natural voice will actually relax and energize you. It will give you more confidence and remove any false armor.

The trick is to find your natural voice—and it's easier than you think. It's so easy, you won't believe it.

Your natural speaking voice can be hidden for any number of reasons. You may have grown up in an era of "children are seen and not heard" and developed what you think is an acceptable voice. You might have an image of what authority looks like and are trying to reach that with your voice. Maybe you developed poor vocal habits and need to learn how to use your voice in a more healthy manner. We'll take a look at the main reasons for not having access to your natural voice in speaking situations: image, breath, and pitch. These insights apply mostly to speaking situations.

Let's start with image. When giving a speech, you might try to project authority. Our image of confidence is often equated with a low, strong voice. A low voice projects gravitas, authority, power, and leadership. Pitching your voice lower than your natural range gives you that Johnny Cash feeling. Remember how he used to open his shows just by coming out and saying, "Hello, I'm Johnny Cash," in that deep baritone voice? The crowd would go crazy. We want the result he got—but using his voice isn't the way to get it.

On the opposite end of the scale, a higher, brighter pitch could imply just that—bright, intelligent, smart. Speaking above your natural range is an attempt to project a clear, nonthreatening, pleasant smartness. These tendencies can fall along gender lines, but not always. I am a female, but rather than pitch my voice up, my nervous habit is to pitch my voice a good octave lower than my most natural voice placement, right into Johnny Cash territory. Why? I have a big personality. Big hair. I'm a big presence. When I get nervous or self-conscious, I try to dial myself back to what my ego tells me is a more reasonable level, so my voice goes low. The reality is that my natural placement is more pleasing and less overwhelming to people because it's genuine. *Take that, ego.*

Is it possible you're trying to project your image of what a leader or speaker should be? Is there an image that comes to mind? Is that image close to who you really are, or are you trying to be like someone you consider successful? It's possible you're reacting to feedback you've gotten from other people. Have you ever been told you're overbearing? Pushy? Have you been told that need to step up, get out there, be confident? What image are you trying to live up to? Think about that, and then get yourself a good Deepak Chopra twenty-one-day meditation and let it go. Who are those people who told you that, and how do they get a vote?

Believe me, the real you has everything you need to make you a compelling speaker. Especially in your voice. Your natural pitch has authority in it. It's inviting. If you don't believe me, then listen to clips of famous news anchors like Ted Koppel,

Barbara Walters, and Walter Cronkite. Try motivational speakers like Tony Robbins, Brené Brown, or Deepak Chopra. They all have, or had, idiosyncratic voices. Unique and real, very much themselves, with what an elocution expert might consider flaws. Instead, they walked into the space of who they were and shared what they had to share by using their natural speaking voice, and we were interested. We'll be interested in you too.

Along with trying to sound like an expert or project an image of authority, we tend to adjust our posture to appear confident. Puffing out our chest like Superman might make us feel strong, but it constricts the diaphragm, which powers the breath. Beveling like a beauty contestant and sucking in your stomach squeezes the air out of your belly. Doing both together may look better in the mirror for a moment, but it's going to tighten the apparatus you have for using your voice, and it will sound fake. Learning how to get your body into proper posture and using your breath to power your voice will make your natural voice not only easier to find but also easier to sustain during a lengthy presentation.

Before you can find your natural pitch for your speaking voice, you need to power up with air. You can learn a lot of in-depth breathing exercises, but quick and easy is always my favorite. Stand up. Plant your feet firmly on the ground. Squeeze your glutes. No really, imagine you're holding a penny between your cheeks. When you do that, your spine lines right up, and that's what you need to access your breath. An aligned spine literally provides you the backbone you need as a speaker.

Now, with your gluts squeezed, release your Superman chest and Miss America stomach suck, and let your belly relax. Then relax the glutes but keep the spine nice and long. Breathe normally through your nose. Do you see your lower belly going in and out? Good. Keep that. Your diaphragm is now doing the work, and you're aligned and ready to find your natural voice.

Your natural voice is about pitch—the notes where your voice naturally falls on the musical scale. Your natural voice lives in a range of pitches. Picture a piano. The black and white keys are the notes. Your natural speaking range is only about three notes, although it might go a little higher when you're excited or lower when you're serious. Our optimal pitch for our speaking voice provides the best way for people to connect with us as speakers. It is a sound that, well, sounds good. It's not pushing or strident. It's not proving or tight with fear. Your voice range of those three notes is where you should live as a speaker. And they are easy to discover.

From your good posture, with your spine aligned, take a nice deep breath through your nose and hum the chorus of "Three Blind Mice." Just those three notes twice: *Mmm, hmm, mmm. Mmm, hmm, mmm.* Stop before you get to "See how they run." Then take a deep breath, hum that last note, and say these words: "One, two, three."

Where you landed for "One, two, three" is your natural pitch. The chorus of "Three Blind Mice" is your natural placement. In fact, those three notes are all the range you need to sound natural and interesting.

I have a pitch pipe app on my phone, and I check the pitch for people in my class. It's best to go individually on this exercise, because if you're in a group, everyone will tune to the group. It's like singing "Happy Birthday" in the office. Everyone might start out on a different note, but by the end, mostly everyone is in unison. That makes it hard to find your own range. Stay solo for this exercise.

My natural pitch is F# above middle C. Without warming up, I gravel out my voice and talk around F below middle C, a full octave below my natural range. But the minute I take a deep breath and hum those first three notes of "Three Blind Mice," my voice pops up where it belongs. It gets clearer. It sounds relaxed and has a clean tone. It's easier to talk all day. In fact, using my natural range, I don't lose my voice if I'm leading a full-day seminar. It's pleasing and easy to listen to in person, on camera, or just on audio in a podcast format.

Use this tool in two ways. First, to discover your pitch and range. Then, before you speak, line up your spine, relax your belly, take a deep breath, and hum those three notes. Great! You're warmed up, settled into your natural voice, and ready to speak all day.

Rhythm and Inflection

You don't need an operatic range to vary your delivery. You don't need more than three notes to make a speech sound interesting or dramatic or to make a point. Using your three-note range won't make you sound monotone. To make your point and add interest, you need rhythm and inflection.

The goal is to get you to your natural best. You can always grow in your timing and delivery. You can take an improv class, an acting class, or a speech class to learn about pace, timing, and nuance, but your baseline natural speaking voice relies on your most natural cadence—which is also something we lose when we're nervous.

A great trick for relaxing into your natural speaking pattern is to read aloud. Words have a rhythm to them. Words strung together in a sentence are accented and unaccented, meaning we push on a word or syllable for meaning. Words have MEAN-ing, they do not have mean-ING. That's the rhythm of language.

Slipping out of a natural cadence and rhythm can happen when you get in front of people and speak. You can go monotone in your delivery or rush the pace, slamming your words together.

If you tend toward monotone, I recommend reading Shakespeare aloud. Because he wrote in iambic pentameter, as you may remember from a long-ago English Lit class, the rhythm is built in. Here's the iambic pentameter rhythm: da DUM, da DUM, da DUM, da DUM, da DUM. There you go. There's your inflection.

One of my favorite speeches to warm up with is the prologue of *Henry V*, not only for its rhythm but also for the language and how it propels you along. Read it aloud and see how it feels. Don't try to be dramatic or act it out. Just read it. Start by taking a deep breath and humming "Three Blind Mice" to get your voice warmed up and ready to go.

> O, for a muse of fire that would ascend
> The brightest heaven of invention!
> A kingdom for a stage, princes to act
> And monarchs to behold the swelling scene![11]

This speech feels like a boat ride on a river to me. It has these ups and downs that flow and move you right along. Try it again, and this time really chew those words and feel how one pushes you to the next: "O" launches you with this nice round vowel that flows into the *m* of muse. "That would ascend" builds naturally, as if you're actually ascending a hill—*would-a-scend.* When you get to the top of that hill, you have these wonderful plosives—*buh* in brightest, *kuh* in kingdom, *geh* in stage, *puh* in princes, *kuh-tuh* in act. Those plosives drive you further up until you get to the *m* in monarchs. A few more plosives—*keh* at the end of monarch and *buh* and *duh* in behold—push you to this wonderful smooth glide, like riding the swell of a wave, into the final declaration of "swelling scene." Try it again now. Deep breath, get your pitch, put yourself in the boat, and feel the ride as you read it aloud. This exercise is like yoga for your voice. You're holding positions and moving from one to the next until you're in flow.

Most poetry has a cadence that can help you slow down. But before you roll your eyes at poetry and Shakespeare, try listening to Billy Collins in his TED talk.[12] A two-time US poet laureate, Billy's poetry, much like his speaking voice, is simple and metered while being insightful and hilarious at the same time. At the end of his TED talk, he reads his poem "To My Favorite 17-Year-Old High School Girl." Notice how he takes his time, using the lines to take breaths. Notice, too, that his range is just a few notes. If you feel like you need to be a bombastic speaker to make an impact, listen to Billy's authentic cadence and tone. Then listen to the uproarious response he gets. This should convince you that simple is better and your authentic voice is best of all. Read one of Billy's poems aloud and see if that doesn't slow you down. Both Shakespeare and Billy will help you command your pace and your breath to help you tell your story with ease.

Another thing that will help you not to slam words together is your enunciation. Actors warm up with tongue twisters and a variety of exercises for the mouth. I have always found it helpful to warm up my plosives: *p*, *b*, *k*, *g*, *t*, and *d*. A simple and silly-sounding warm-up is to say those plosives each three times: *Puh-puh-puh, buh-buh-buh, tuh-tuh-tuh, duh-duh-duh, kuh-kuh-kuh, guh-guh-guh.* That will get your tongue and lips warmed up and keep you from tripping on your words. If you have difficulty with a particular consonant, say an *s* or a *c*, find a tongue twister that uses those letters, and say it aloud a few times.

The final thing you should read aloud is your own speech. Your elevator pitch. Your mission statement. If it's something you're going to say to an individual or a group, especially when there are stakes, like trying to get a client or a job, you need to know what it sounds like coming out of your mouth. You need to know what it feels like, what words pop, where you rush, where you need to pick up the pace, where you lose inflection or run out of air.

Train your vocal instrument on your natural pitch and in a natural cadence, and you'll have all the gravitas and power you need to be your genuine self and connect with your audience.

Takeaways:

✓ Your goal for a presentation is not perfection or sales or applause. It's about connection.

✓ Master your nerves in public speaking by being relaxed and energized.

✓ Move or don't move—make it a choice.

✓ Make eye contact with your audience using the three-second Swedish *skol* approach.

Chapter 8

Take the Stage

Making Friends

The majority of the shows I performed with the World Showcase Players at Epcot were three-person shows. Three actors used a well-known story and plucked guests from the audience to play the main characters. In the years I spent with this troupe, we experimented with the best times and places to perform our shows. We were pretty mobile. We had no stage or lights—just us and a cart filled with props—so we could go anywhere.

One of our experiments was early in the day in the Italy pavilion. If you've ever been to Epcot, then you know it's about a half-mile walk from the front of the park, where the big ball is, to the next part of the park with the countries. World Showcase is a giant circular walkway

157

that surrounds a lagoon, with Canada to the right and Mexico to the left. It's one-and-a-half miles around the lagoon, with Italy close to the halfway mark.

In those days, World Showcase didn't open until eleven. Guests would start their day in the first part of the park, riding rides. Then at eleven, they'd meander from country to country, eating, shopping, and sometimes playing the "drinking around the world" game. A guest following this typical pattern would make it to Italy around one in the afternoon. Usually our first show in Italy was at two, by which time tired guests were ready to park themselves and enjoy some entertainment.

One spring, we were asked to start our shows in Italy at eleven thirty. Anyone who wanted to see that show would need to seriously move to get there on time. How many people do you imagine were committed to the eleven thirty World Showcase Players' show printed on their map? I'd say the average number was three, possibly less—and remember, we always picked three guests to be in the show. That means this experiment was bound to fail, but we needed to try it, if for no other reason than that it was scheduled.

On the second day of the experiment, our cast included me and Mark Daniel. Mark was then a stand-up comic and actor. He has since gone on to become the warm-up host for *Star Wars* events, hosting George Lucas and Harrison Ford and leading Q&As for fans. He's also the host of *Disney Parks Live*. He entertains crowds of hundreds, even thousands, at events like the Walt Disney World Christmas Parade.

That day in Italy, the plan was for me to tell the story and for Mark to do the pre-show. The goal of the pre-show is to get the audience ready to interact in the show and to make enough cheering sounds to gather an even larger crowd. Most days, we came out to crowds of twenty to fifty. During the holidays, we could pack the street with two to three hundred. This day, we entered the Italian pavilion to find three audience members.

Mark looked at me and said, "We need to cancel. We can't do this." I looked up the lane and saw a couple in American Adventure. Scanning the lagoon, I saw a few more families walking around. "I think we're good," I said. "We have enough people to start. Let's do it."

Mark's eyes got really big, but I started to set up, and we greeted the three people who were there to see the show. They had their maps and their showtime guide. They clearly planned on seeing this show. Mark got more and more agitated as we set up, and I got more and more calm. Finally he said to me, "Okay, I can't do this. I don't know how to start this show with just three people."

Now, I started my performing career with SAK Theatre, one of the comedy troupes that built an interactive style in the 1970s at Renaissance festivals. They taught me to love the audience and make them the star. I knew how to do this. I had learned to adapt to audiences and had many times started performances with just a few people in the audience at the Michigan Renaissance Faire.

"I really think we can do it," I said. "What about if we switch—you tell the story, and I'll do the warm-up. I'll get these people ready, and I bet we'll get ten people."

With our new plan, Mark headed out. His job now would be to stand out on the walkway and hawk the show, letting people know it was going on. I started my part, which was to connect with each of the three people there.

I drew in really close, tailoring jokes to them and making it an intimate experience while never letting down my performance energy. It was like a slightly elevated conversation. I couldn't let it get casual, but I also couldn't perform full out. I was more like a coach in the huddle, pumping up my team, than a performer on a stage. We joked and bantered. We built a rapport. I never looked up to see if more people were coming. My focus was fully on my team of three.

A pre-show usually lasts three to five minutes. I was going to take longer—six to seven, maybe. As we huddled, other people stopped to see what we were doing. Once they did, we included them. But I never stopped what I was doing or tried to get others to join us. The pre-show ended as it usually did, with me getting the crowd to clap and cheer wildly. "Go crazy!" I said. The tiny but engaged crowd did clap and cheer and go crazy in their fun, cute, bonded way.

The show started properly when the two other players ran in. Mark told the story to a group of about ten. Maybe we got up to twelve during the show.

It was a fine show. Not disastrous, not terrific, but fun—and the three people who planned their day around that early show left happy. As we walked backstage, Mark told me he didn't go out and hawk the crowd during the pre-show. Instead, he stood inside the shop entrance, watching.

"I got it now," he said. "I saw what you did. I can do this tomorrow."

What did I do? I made those three people my friends. I gave them my full attention and didn't worry about the numbers we should have had. I didn't even worry about the people walking by. If they stopped, they stopped, and if not, that was fine. I planned to have a good time with these three happy friends. Our intimate connection was the draw to the other seven people walking by. They wanted what we had. They wanted to be part of the fun group. If I'd looked past my three new friends and tried to focus on making more friends, I would have lost the three and not gained the seven.

The energy I had in the pre-show was at a level for three people interested in a show. Too relaxed and it would have been a chat that wouldn't have gotten us to show-level energy or gained us more audience members. Too energized and it would have blown those three people away and made them uncomfortable.

Your delivery must be genuine and true to you and to the situation. This goes for in-person and online promotions as well. If you focus on the followers you don't have or the numbers you think you need to gain, you'll lose the followers you do have. But when you create a connection with the people you have, other people will naturally want to find out what's going on, and that genuine interaction will draw them in.

Mark did the show the next morning, and it was great. He's a truly kind and funny fellow, and audiences love him. He applied this principle to his work once we moved to a better show time, and his pre-shows were winners. Do I take credit for him going on to become a well-known warm-up host in the *Star Wars* universe? Of course I do. Just as I hope to take some measure of credit for your success when you apply this principle to your audience interactions.

Make an Offer

Taking the stage can be terrifying because of the reason you're taking the stage. When you take the stage, either in person or in an online post, you're making an ask. You're asking your audience to invest in you, in your idea, or in your company. You're asking them to buy what you're selling.

There's an easier way to take the stage than coming in cold and making an ask. Instead, you can read the energy of the room and make an offer—an invitation—to your audience. When you can read the energy of the room, you can guide it.

When you first try to engage with an audience, their energy and your energy may start in two different places. You need to learn to read both, which you can then combine to create a new energy you can guide. When your delivery is genuine and true to you and the situation, you create an energy level that draws people in. Your ultimate goal in your relationship with your audience is to make a sale or solicit a donation. This is clear and therefore not manipulative when you guide the energy toward that conclusion.

In the pre-show in Italy, my goal was to get more people. I said this up front to the three people I started with. There was no confusion about the intention of our relationship. I took the energy of the audience where they were, which I would say was interested, and boosted it to excited in a step-by-step way. First, I invited them to the next level of energy, which was my own level of energy: anticipatory. When they got there, I could guide them to the next level. Maybe that level was motivated to see the show. Anytime another person joined, we celebrated: "Ooh! We're almost there! We're getting closer to starting the show! Let's see if we can entice two more people, and then we'll start!" Eventually, we all arrived at cheering and clapping, excited to start the show.

When you start cold, you need to warm the room. Warm the audience. Figure out where they are. Are they indifferent? Move them to curious. Do they start curious? Take them to interested. Interested? Move to anticipatory. On and on up the ladder.

In audience participation theater, the most important element to a successful show is obvious: the audience. They are a member of the cast. My view was always that the more the audience did in the show, the better the show would be. That's why it was important to warm them up, getting them ready to play their part.

I still feel this way about an audience. I recently did a ninety-minute presentation for the company I work with in Thailand. Originally, the presentation was scheduled for ten people, the executive team. The leaders were excited about the event, though, and started including their teams. We ended up with a presentation for seventy-five. All my plans for an interactive session went out the window. My session was now a large audience, all of whom had English as a second language and some of whom weren't totally comfortable with English. Most everyone was Thai, a culture notoriously kind and hospitable. I knew they would be looking at me with total attention, even if they were bored or confused.

Even in this situation, I applied the principle that the audience was the most important element in my presentation, and I expected to get them to a place where they were doing just as much, if not more, than I was. To do that, I view the audience as a living, breathing organism and my job as a caretaker. I invite them to join me, and it's my responsibility to continually feed and care for them. In order to go from a cold room to a warmed-up audience, you need to take their temperature. By reading them as one personality, you can evaluate what they're offering, affirm it and then bring them to the next level.

My approach is a step-up approach. I don't come into a cold room and expect them to go from disjointed to cheering and screaming. If they're quiet, the next level might be anticipatory. If they're disjointed, I want to unify them. If they're disinterested, I want to take them to curious. If they're connected and ready to dive in, I want to take them to exuberant. If I come in to a boisterous, exuberant crowd, I want to grab hold of that energy, control it by giving it a focus, and then knock it out of the park.

Take the pressure off yourself to bring Tony Robbins energy to every room with every audience. Figure out their energy, and then step them up the ladder to the best spot for them to receive your offer. You can do this in your online communication with your audience as well. Are they responding to your posts? Are they engaging with your emails? Rather than start with "Donate now," start with "Did you know?" See what kind of response you get. Then invite them deeper.

In my event in Thailand, I started with a polite and kind group of people and stepped them up the ladder to warmly engaged until we got to energized. Following the event, many individuals shared with me what they got out of the presentation. I could tell they had engaged their imaginations and started applying what we did to their business unit. That was audience interaction style for me, even though we didn't do any exercises. None of them got up and spoke or participated by sharing their responses, as I would have invited with a group of ten. Still, they engaged their minds and participated through their individual responses.

Yes, And

One of the rules in improvisation is making an offer. Improvisors experience unexpected situations in real time. If you've seen *Whose Line Is It Anyway?* or any live improv show, then you've seen this principle in action. A good example is the game where four contestants stand, two and two, on either side of the stage. The host tosses out a suggestion, and one of the players jumps from the sidelines to center stage and starts the scene. Other players from either side then jump in and join the scene by making an offer.

The first improvisor might have started a scene driving a car. That's an offer. Ryan Stiles is in a car, driving. Here comes Wayne Brady. He gets into the back seat of the car and says, "To the airport, and step on it." Wayne has taken the offer of a car and added to it that Ryan is a taxi driver.

This is the famous "Yes, And" that you've likely heard about, and it's similar to the "Yes, Let's" exercise we did in an earlier chapter. The offer is presented. The person who takes the offer says yes to it—in this case, driving in the car—and adds another offer, such as making it a taxi drive to the airport. Wayne could have gotten in the front seat of the car and said, "Dad, we're late for school!" This would have been a totally different offer. It would still have been a yes to the car and Ryan as a driver, but with an addition of "I'm your son and you're driving me to school."

As a presenter on stage or on the page, you're making an offer to your audience. You've memorized your talking points and know your stories, but you're making an offer in real time and getting an unrehearsed reaction from your audience. Sometimes it can feel like you're pressuring your audience. You have a sale to make. You have a donation to solicit. Flip this script from a request that demands an answer to making a genuine offer. To connect with your audience by making an offer, you need to create the environment of "Yes, And."

You are, after all, offering an opportunity. It is a genuine offer. You have information or instruction to share, which might come in the form of a speech if you're a subject-matter expert. You know the product you sell will help your customer make more money or lose more weight. A nonprofit's offer might be to participate in your mission, to change the face of your community, or to support the work you're doing on their behalf. View these "asks" as offers. Yes, you're asking for their money or resources to be applied to your organization. You're also offering an opportunity. Your offer is beneficial for their lives. Your organization or your product or service will help them survive and thrive.

In my pre-show at Walt Disney World, I wasn't just taking from them. I wasn't just demanding they cheer so I could check this show off the list and keep my job. I was offering them a show—an interactive, fun show that would create a magical memory for them and their family: "Remember that time we were in Epcot and we were the only ones there for the show? And somehow we got more people to come and it was so funny? That was so cool!" I had a gift to give them, just as I needed them to make my business work.

Approach it as an offer, and you're giving your audience the opportunity to respond and participate instead of hunting for a one-off sale. An offer comes with a sense of space. There's space for the recipient to receive the offer. You invite them to engage and use the offer in a way that will benefit them.

Give a Gift

Another exercise we do in our classes is an improv warm-up called "Give a Gift." Everyone gets in a circle, and one person starts by handing an imaginary gift to the person on their right. Then we all watch as the recipient pretends to open the gift. When she opens it, she gets to make it whatever she wants: "A plant for my desk. How thoughtful." Then she mimes wrapping it back up and gives the gift to the person to her right. He opens it and says, "Wow! Two tickets to Paris—this is perfect!" He wraps it up and passes the gift for the next person to open.

We do this because it's a fun icebreaker and loosens us up. It also has a lesson to teach us, which is that when we make an offer, we can't be sure how it will be received. We can't control how our client or audience will apply the offer. With this exercise, the muscle we're warming up is our ability to offer something without knowing how it will be received.

When you offer something that's important or precious to you, like your mission statement, your resumé, or your proposal, the energy with which you hand it over can sometimes be gripping: "You NEED to hire me!" This exercise helps us train that muscle to release that grip.

In the game I just described, you might imagine the gift you're giving is one thing (an orchid, a plane ticket) and then watch what someone else discovers when they open it. It takes practice to defer judgment on how your gift should be used, but this practice helps you learn to let your gift become an offer. The energy shift from "Make this work for me," "Hire me," or "Buy my product" to "Here, I made this for you so you'll grow and become more successful" is palpable.

You can apply this approach to written content as well. When you send out an email asking your followers to purchase your product, think about how you're offering something that will benefit them. Would you send out an email that said, "Buy this book so I can pay my rent?" Of course not. You believe in your services—that they will truly make your clients' lives better. Your product will help them survive and thrive. It's a generous offer. Take that approach and make your ask about the audience and their needs, rather than about you and your needs. They'll respond when your offer supports their ability to survive and thrive. If it only supports your thriving and surviving, why should they care?

Read the Energy

Listening to the energy of the room is a fine-tuned part of the craft of a speaker. There's an energy in the room, and it's your job to gather it and transform it into the energy that best suits your offer. Sometimes you can be successful at this, and sometimes the audience resists.

There were occasions in my work as an actor at Walt Disney World that on a Friday evening, I would portray the Fairy Godmother in the castle restaurant, then on the following Saturday afternoon perform a comedy show in the Italian pavilion at Epcot. These are two vastly different experiences, with totally different audiences and sets of expectations.

The Friday night audience had saved up, made a reservation, and was literally in the most magical spot in the most magical place on earth. They were waiting for magic to happen, with responses of "Oh, look! Here's comes the Fairy Godmother, and she's singing 'Bibbidi Bobbidi Boo' to me! This is the best day ever!" Conversely, at one in the afternoon on a Saturday at Epcot, guests have often been drinking around the world. Remember how Italy is about halfway through that world? Remember that this is in Florida, and that we're performing outside? Sweaty, tired guests now felt themselves accosted by entertainment.

One Saturday afternoon, as I entered shouting "Showtime!" a man responded by cursing at me. He just wanted to sit there, and I'd interrupted his moment. This was a marked difference from the evening before, when I made my entrance to hear a child calling out, "I love you, Fairy Godmother!"

It's good to listen to the energy in the room and agree with it in either situation. Remember "Yes, And." Yes, I love you too, and I'm going to sing for you. Yes, I want you to sit here as well, and I'm going to entertain in this space while you rest. In my experience, the important thing is to continue to offer. You have no idea how your offer will travel with a person, even a resistant one. Perhaps it will sand down the rough edges, making way for them to see your offer of a solution to a problem. It could be days, even months, later. You have no idea if that rude person had a bad sandwich and just wanted to get to their bottle of Tums. Maybe they had a fight with their spouse on the way out the door. You don't know. So offer, and let the offer do the work.

The Lingering Ring

I've had job interviews where I walked into the room and felt an electric current connecting me and the person conducting the interview, even though we had never met. Who can know why? By reading the room, I'm able to relax into it and agree that yes, this energy is us together. We belong together.

I've also walked into rooms where my energy was too nervous or needy. In those cases, I wasn't able to read the energy of those in the room and make the connection. Other times, I could tell the room was distracted or against me. In some cases, I've been able to turn my nerves or their distracted energy around with a "Yes, And." I'd relax, breathe in a calm way, make eye contact, and let them know I was listening to them. When you meet an audience at their point of distraction or resistance, you can move the energy to something else—from distracted to anticipatory or from resistant to interested. It's all about communicating "Yes, I see you and I hear you, and I have this to offer."

What happens when this doesn't work? When you can't move the energy of the room? One job I should have had—it was mine; I'd been working there on a project for ten months and was grooving with everyone there—didn't happen. I walked into a room with their panel of ten people, and I knew. They'd gone a different direction. Even before I sat down, I knew.

In these cases, I like to approach it like the goodbye song on *American Idol* or *The Voice*. You know, when a singer must "sing for their life" or "sing for America's votes." There are usually three singers and only one spot. At that point, each singer needs to give the most generous, gracious performance of their life. If you don't get the votes—and let's face it, we all know which of the three is getting the votes—what you want is a moment, a snapshot of who you are, a performance that rings like a bell. You know how when you ring a bell and even when the hammer stops hitting it, it continues to ring? That's what you want— a lingering ring of your offering.

They've gone a different direction, and even though you won't change their mind in that moment, you want your energy to hang around. You want to leave a positive echo in their memory, especially when they find themselves in a meeting later, looking for a solution. You want them to be able to say, "You know what we need? We need that Disney lady." Or "We need that idea that organization brought us…" Or "What about doing an event where all the proceeds go to that group—you remember, that guy that did the presentation three years ago?"

I know it seems like it will never happen, but it does. My dad was the head of the Naval Base Reuse Commission in Orlando, Florida, leading the redesign of what that massive plot of land would become: a new neighborhood called Baldwin Park. While the commission entertained proposals, a bunch of old base buildings hung around empty. Coincidentally, Tom Hanks and Steven Spielberg were about to shoot their HBO miniseries *From the Earth to the Moon*, and they were looking for a bunch of old military-looking rooms in which to film.

For many months that year, my dad was the point person for their production manager, a huge guy named Ivan with long hair and turquoise rings. They made quite a pair, my retired navy captain dad and this production manager, but my dad decided anything the production company needed, he would get them. Ivan would call, and my dad would head down to the closed base and open something up and get the lights turned on. He was invited to lunch on the set with Tom Hanks. He was invited out to the Kennedy Space Center to watch a launch. He had a great time.

Years later, Hanks and Spielberg were in a meeting in Hollywood, talking about another project, *Band of Brothers*. They were in the planning stages and trying to figure out locations. They needed to create a barracks and shoot the first few episodes of the soldiers in boot camp. Someone at the meeting said,

"What about that guy? That guy in Orlando. The navy guy. He might have a connection." My dad got a call from Ivan, who said, "Your name came up in a meeting with Spielberg and Hanks. Can you help us?"

You can hear it, can't you? *Ring.* Steven Spielberg and Tom Hanks have very full lives and have met and worked with many hundreds of people in the years that followed *From the Earth to the Moon.* But the lingering energy of a single person's offer and connection remained.

That's your job. Ring your own bell, and let the vibration follow.

Count to Ten

How do you feel that energy vibration? An exercise we do in my workshops requires a larger group of people. We divide them into smaller groups of five or ten, and they're asked to form a circle, like a football huddle. In each huddle, there's a moderator.

The group is asked to look at the ground, not each other, and their task is to count to ten. That's all. Just count to ten. Only you don't know who'll start. You don't know who'll say two or three or eight. The rules are, you can't indicate. You can't start a pattern or go in an order. If two people say the same number at the same time, you start again. The moderator stops and restarts the group if that happens, or if they notice a pattern or indications going on.

In this exercise, you must feel the energy of the group. And you'll feel it not only in the group, but in yourself. You'll know "I have number four." The energy to say four will bubble up in you. You'll also feel the energy of the person who has number three. Sometimes you'll get it wrong and two people will say a number at the same time. But at some point you'll get into a groove of the energy and your team will count from one to ten, just feeling it.

We do this exercise once with no timeline, no pressure. Just count to ten. Then we do it a second time and make it a competition. Whichever team gets to ten first wins a prize. That changes the energy in the room very quickly.

It's a useful exercise for people who've never had to read a room or aren't sure how the energy in a room can differ or shift. Once you feel the energy of someone getting ready to say three without looking at them, you now have a baseline for what energy feels like. You can apply that to any room you enter to share your story, be it a board room or a convention hall.

Underscore

Here's a solo energy exercise—one I call underscoring. The underscore in a movie or TV show captures the energy of the scene and drives what's going on. I'm always listening for the underscore of a meeting when I speak. Is this room on a jazz score? Hip hop? Orchestral? What's the beat of the energy here?

You can practice feeling the underscore by choosing a movie you've watched before and putting it on mute. Without the sound on, let yourself feel the energy of the scene, where it's going, the expression of the actors. Then rewind and put on the sound. What music played underneath that scene? Does it match the energy you felt? Did you connect to that energy without hearing it? Try this with different movie genres—suspense, romance, comedy, drama, action, slapstick comedy—to build your muscle for feeling an underscore before you hear it.

Try a run-through of your talk with music playing underneath. Try underscoring your mission statement. Play with different types of music and see what fits best. Then you can carry that energy with you when you speak.

Stage Map

Now that we've addressed the woo-woo energy of presenting, it's time to get practical. How do you actually present your material? Where do you stand? What do you do with your hands? Should you memorize your talk or not? What if you mess up?

Taking the stage isn't just getting up and standing there. It's about owning the space and owning your right to present what you came there to say. And believe it or not, where you stand can help give you power. Some places on stage give you strength, and some places make you weak. When you understand where the stronger places are, you can give yourself a strong position, whether you're leading a meeting in a conference room or giving a speech from a platform.

The stage for theater productions is broken into a grid. This is so the director, who's standing out in the house where the audience sits, can call out directions to the actors and they'll know where to go: "That was lovely, dear. Now could you possibly get up on the line and cross stage right, then hit center just at the end? Eddie, you'll follow from up left until you meet her center. All good? Wonderful, let's go again." If you don't know your stage map, you would wander lost at those directions.

The stage map is from the point of view of the actor on the stage looking to the audience. Right is the actor's right. Left the actor's left. Center is the exact middle of the stage. When you face an audience, you want to use your right, left, and center as your map.

You can apply this map to a full stage in a conference hall with ten thousand people in attendance at your speech. You can also see the grid under your feet when standing at the podium in a conference room with a table and whiteboard behind you.

Center is always the strongest spot. It's where we take all directions to find the best spot. Downstage is the closest zone to the audience, and down right is the second strongest spot onstage. Stepping from center to down right is very strong positioning. Upstage is always the weakest spot because upstage, or up of center, is the farthest point from the audience.

If you're giving a talk in a small room, put the podium to your center left, with the screen at center behind you. When you move away from the podium, you're headed center and right— the strongest places. If you plan to stand at the podium without moving, place it center right. Remember—move or don't move. When we get nervous, we tend to float upstage a bit. We're hiding, but casually. Don't wander upstage to a very weak position. Your point will be lost. If you're going to move, move right to the center and then back to your podium.

Memorizing

Maybe you think great speakers have their talks memorized. If you've watched many TED speakers, you could certainly be left with that impression. And there are situations where you need to have memorized your story. The elevator pitch won't work if you have to pull out a three-by-five card or the notes on your smartphone to read it to people—that is, unless the elevator is stuck and you're there for a while and the other passengers are willing to listen.

A memorized speech offers a level of professionalism, but the real secret is that a great speaker is an authentic speaker. The writer Anne Lamott gave a talk at the TED2017 conference titled "Twelve Truths I Learned from Life and Writing"[13]—and she read her list of twelve things. She stood at a podium, just reading it, and it was riveting. She's a writer and goes to many appearances where people want her to read from her books. She's not a speaker like Tony Robbins. Her audience wasn't expecting her to run around the stage. They were fully engaged as she read.

I would bet she also "memorized" the piece. By that, I mean she knew the flow. She likely practiced it and understood where the beats were. The beats are the places to pause, to take in the energy of the audience, to give them room to breathe and for them to respond and laugh. She may have read it, but she still knew it.

Whether you read, use notes on a podium, reference a teleprompter, or have totally memorized your talk, you need to know the material. You need to have confidence that if you lose your place, the power goes out on the teleprompter, or you go blank and forget everything, you can find your way back to your content.

Here is a tried-and-true technique for helping you memorize your speech and solidify the content in your mind:

1. Write the entire speech out as a story. Write every word. Commas for breath. Line breaks for pauses. Write it all like it's an article about to be published.

2. Then outline the article. Just like you were taught in fourth grade, with Roman numerals and capital letters. Put the keywords from each paragraph as the headers in your outline.
3. Highlight the keywords in those headers.
4. Read your speech out loud, verbatim, from the article first.
5. Then stand up and practice your speech holding your outline, not the fully written speech. Fill in the gaps for yourself without looking at the article version.
6. Memorize your outline. Get yourself from keyword to keyword as you move through it.

By writing it out as a full speech, you trick your body. You kinetically store the words in your brain through your fingers, which moved while you wrote. If you just jot notes for your speech or use the notes section of PowerPoint, you don't know what you might say. Your brain hasn't been imprinted with concrete information. When you write it out, your brain sees it and your body translates the information from your fingers through your joints to your spine, up and into your cortex.

When you write it the second time, in outline form, your brain takes a picture of that outline. Here again, your body helps your brain by moving your hand across the keys or the pen across the page. You solidify the speech when you stand up and speak it out loud, just from those key words. You train your brain to fill in the gaps. Even if you go blank and can't remember what you wrote, you'll know what to say. You can talk your way from keyword to keyword.

If you need to, you can put some keywords and headings into your PowerPoint notes or on a notecard. You can glance at it, but you'll know your speech. You'll have it in your brain and in your body. You could get from one keyword to the next keyword if all the technology disappeared and all that was left was you and the audience.

Stage or Page

When you put yourself in charge of your own system, you master your nerves. You can be genuine in your delivery and true to you and the situation because you won't be hijacked by fight, flight, or freeze. Relaxed and energized, you'll use your natural voice in the energy and flow that's right for you and the room. And the good news is, you can apply the principles of this chapter and the previous one to your brand voice on the page as well. When you know your genuine voice, you can recognize it in writing.

I recently took some web design courses to help me launch the new version of my website. I got a little lost in groove of the teacher's voice and wrote headers like "Get Results Now!" and "Your Key to Success Here!" I lost my brand voice and adopted theirs.

To re-find my voice, I took a deep breath and put on some music that I consider my brand playlist. It has songs like "Happy" by Pharrell Williams and "Can't Stop the Feeling!" by Justin Timberlake and anything by the Talking Heads or Stevie Nicks. Then I reminded myself of the purpose of taking the class. They wanted me to hook *my* audience. To show them the value of *my* offer. I centered in on my genuine voice to discover the headers that accomplished that outcome—but in my own brand voice, not theirs.

Takeaways:

✓ Focus on the audience in front of you.

✓ Your delivery must be genuine and true to you and the situation.

✓ Meet the audience's energy and guide them to your intended outcome with a step-by-step approach.

✓ As a presenter on stage or on the page, you're making an offer to your audience. You're giving them the opportunity to respond and participate in a way that benefits them.

✓ Ring your own bell, and let the vibration follow.

✓ Center stage is the strongest spot, and down right is second. If you move, keep to these zones.

✓ Whether you memorize your speech or not, you need to know the material.

Chapter 9

Tell Your Story

My Dream Job

Underneath the streets of the Magic Kingdom are its famous tunnels called the Utilidor. The tunnels connect each of the different lands and allow cast members to travel between them without breaking the continuity of the story. For example, you won't ever see a shop host from Tomorrowland, dressed in a space-age costume, walking through the streets of Frontierland.

I loved being in the Utilidor—especially during the extended period of time I was "friends" with the Fairy Godmother. It felt like the biggest backstage in the world, and for me there's just nothing better than being backstage, getting ready to go on. Even better, I wore a big, floaty, blue gown with a bright pink bow. I was fully immersed in a magical character and I loved it.

Now, the Utilidor is not the most magical place in the world. Picture concrete walls with exposed pipes; golf carts filled with boxes driving through; and people just back from lunch, costumes in hand. But because I was there for a limited engagement, I lived out my fantasy world as the Fairy Godmother both backstage and onstage. After the show, I didn't take off my hood or wig or gloves. I floated through tunnels, waving at cast members on their way to their shifts. I sang. I skipped. I waved at the security cameras if I was alone. Maintenance workers stopped to give me rides on their golf carts as I traveled from my dressing room to the restaurant for the show, and I would wave from the golf cart like I was in the parade. I became smitten with the opportunity to bring this magical character to life wherever I went.

One woman I saw every day worked in Tomorrowland. I passed her in the tunnel on my way from my first show on my first day. She was red faced, sweating, and tired. She had just come from moving strollers, and she was beat. I stopped and chatted with her, asking, "How are you, my dear?" She told me about the day she was having, and I thanked her for taking care of the guests.

I was authentically interested in her, both as Alice and the Fairy Godmother. I used some of the language of my character. ("My dear" isn't how I normally address team members.) But I was also talking to her about our guests, which was not something my character would have been aware of—but Alice, an almost-fifteen-year Disney employee, was. I was in the brand story and my own story.

Every day, we chatted until it was my last week. I told her I would be heading back to Epcot and invited her to stop by if she was there. She thanked me for taking time with her and said she appreciated that I enjoyed the magic and wanted to extend it past my onstage duties.

It was a pick-me-up for her and helped her get back into the magic of her own tasks.

Telling your story in a variety of mediums requires you to know your larger brand story and apply it to specific, smaller situations. In my case, with this story, I knew the story of the brand, which was Walt Disney World. The brand story for Walt Disney World is "We Create Happiness." That's the job of every cast member, from the CEO to the Fairy Godmother to the attraction host at Space Mountain.

I also knew my specific story inside the brand story at that moment. I was dressed as the Fairy Godmother, walking down a corridor. I could have taken off the wig and been kind and still applied myself to "We Create Happiness." Of course that would have worked. But how much more effective was it for me to lean into the moment, to approach this tired worker as the Fairy Godmother and ask her how she was doing? If I was Alice, wearing a white T-shirt, holding a wig, and carrying a coffee cup, and said "How are you?" the woman likely would have said "Great" and kept going. Being in a specific situation, I applied the bigger story and created more connection.

You have stories to tell. Many stories. Stories of the victories you've helped others achieve. Stories of your impact on your community. Stories of your services and products bringing real change to your customers. You also have stories of overcoming. You have wisdom to share that will help others to survive and thrive. When you tell your stories, you build trust with your audience.

I said this before—telling your story is hard. You aren't crazy. Crafting a good story is hard! It's harder than a formula, even though we've been talking about the Story Formula in this book. There is mystery to a great story. Have you ever seen a speaker come off a stage and be surprised by how well the audience reacted? You may have even experienced it yourself. There is a bit of magic outside the formula, and that magic is you—your deeper intention and the passion you bring to your business.

The mysterious and magical interchange of energy between you and your audience can't be found in a formula or template. Those things help, but you need to find the magic that's unique to you. The purpose of this final chapter is for you to go from a formulaic approach to your messaging to embracing the storyteller within. This will help you craft unique, meaningful messages that create a bond between you and your audience.

Two Stories

There are two stories you need to know and you need to tell. One doesn't change, and one changes constantly. The first is the brand story, the one narrative that tells everyone who you are and what you're about. Then under the umbrella of that brand story, you have daily stories—examples and messages that remind your audience of your bigger narrative. Those daily stories hook your audience into the larger story.

We're going to start with the larger brand story—the one narrative that ties all those tales together. You have a universal theme everyone can relate to and specific details that hook their interest. Your job is to use the tools you've found in this book to find that narrative. What is the universal theme that drives you and your organization? What is the story you have to tell? Like the story "We Create Happiness" at Disney, what is the story that infuses every interaction you have in what you do?

Activate Your Mission

There are some who would say the brand story is the same thing as a vision or a mission, or even a core value. Any of those concepts are great to guide your business plan. But when you can turn that vision or mission into a narrative loop that you and your employees want to live inside—and, even better, that your customers are interested in being a part of too—then you have a brand story.

Why is "We Create Happiness" a story? It meets all of our criteria for a story. It's universal so everyone can relate to it. It's specifically enacted in millions of interactions daily. It has action— look at the words "we create." And it's a story that everyone at Disney, whether they're a cast member or guest, wants to be part of.

Take your mission statement or your vision and see if you can activate it. Literally, ask yourself and your team, "What does this vision look like in action?" When you see activities and behaviors that express your vision, you can start to see the story of your brand.

Don't follow the trail many businesses do of thinking your origin story is your brand story. It's not. Your origin story belongs in the "about" section of your website. In my case, it's the blue Dodge Dart story. It might be the story you tell in speeches. It's the "we started in a garage" story that tells the origins of how, when, and where you started it all. And it's a great story—or at least it's great now that you have to tools to craft it and make it great. But that's not the story I'm talking about.

Your brand story is the story of the problem you solve. As a business, you solve a problem. You meet a need. And you need to know that story because it forms the umbrella under which all the other stories go. It's like the big umbrella on our porch that we've strung with colored lights. The umbrella forms the structure for all the little points of light that illuminate the entire deck.

Walt drawing Mickey Mouse for the first time on a train is an origin story, but "We Create Happiness" is a brand story. It's the one you post on the wall of your office and on the front of the employee handbook. It's the one printed on the company ID cards we show the security guards every day, reminding us of who we are. We create happiness. That's what we do. We're not trying to create magic or be magical or make everything perfect. We use magical stories and imaginative play to create happiness. That's all we're looking to do. I can do that in any context—as a custodian on Main Street, as an ice cream vendor, or as the Fairy Godmother in the castle.

As an employer, the Walt Disney Company can trust me to tell that story and deliver on that promise in my own way through the role I perform at my location. They don't have to oversee every step of it or make sure that in my role as a holiday storyteller, I'm telling the same story as the ticket agent at the front of the park. We're both telling the same story. We create happiness. With that knowledge, we can go on about our business of making those daily stories work for the individual guests we encounter all day long.

You can do that too. You can create a strong brand narrative and empower your team with the tools in this book so they tell your story in every situation they face. In their day-to-day tasks, they'll share the story of your brand. They can also bring you examples you can craft into those daily supporting stories of the brand story.

What's the difference between a brand story and your supporting stories? Take a look at my universal brand story and the supporting stories used in this book to help you get the picture. My brand story is: "Most businesses have a great story—they just don't know how to tell it. I help leaders find, craft, and deliver the right story for each moment. Because when you tell a story that connects, you build trust with your audience and grow your business. When you understand the ancient power of story, you inspire others and call them to action." In one sentence, my brand story is "I activate the power of story."

I don't tell this brand story everywhere I go. In fact, I rarely ever tell this story. It lives on my website and is the introduction I offer when I meet someone who asks, "What do you do?" It serves as my elevator pitch. This brand story guides me to know what stories to tell that support the overarching story. You've read many of my supporting stories in this book:

- Feliz Navidad, Mickey
- The audience warm-up with Mark Daniel
- Training pastors at a megachurch
- The Fairy Godmother in the Utilidor
- My son's catchphrase, "I'm thinking about me!"
- Traveling across country with my dad, listening to stories (my origin story)

The reason I don't tell my brand story is because I use the supporting stories to show my brand story. It's how I live the "Show, Don't Tell" rule—and you can do it too.

Share the Love

To discover your brand story, use the story tools we've already established with a focus on your audience. Your audience is full of the people you want to serve. You have a passion for them. Start by thinking about them and why you care about their problem.

Here are some fill-in-the-blank statements you can answer about your audience, or your ideal customer, that will help you discover your one-sentence brand story:

1. I love my customer/audience because:
2. Their specific problem is:
3. Their universal need is:
4. I help them meet that need and overcome their specific problem by:
5. I do this because:

Here are the responses I wrote to help me shape my own brand story. See if this helps you craft your own.

1. I love my customer/audience because of what they are trying to do—share their passion for their vision and mission with people who will give them money to keep doing it. They need to share their story with staff who want to help and will help more if they know why. With the world, because they're doing something powerful and amazing and everyone needs to know about it.

2. Their specific problem is they're the go-to for every-thing in their business. Whether they're just starting out or have a small team, they're the one with the passion and the vision. They're the engine that fuels their organization. That means they need to write the tweet, approve the brochure, be the spokesperson, meet with the donors or clients, and do the payroll. They're overwhelmed with the details, and they don't know how to find the best story to tell. They may just be telling the origin story over and over, hoping for the best.

It's also likely they're not naturally gifted speakers or writers. That's not what they started their business to do. Nonprofits got started to serve the special needs community, have a place for artists to perform, feed hungry kids, or get scholarships to girls on the brink. Businesses got started because they had a passion for health and fitness, for art supplies, or for baking.

Before they step up to a podium or sit down to write a post, they're wondering, "Is what I'm about to say going to connect?" They don't know how to tell their story or how to get their people to tell their story because they don't have the tools. They don't know how to maintain brand standards if each team member adds their own personality to the stories they tell, so they just do it all.

3. Their universal need is they need to be seen and heard. They need to connect.

4. I help them meet that need and overcome their specific problem by helping them tell their story. By giving them tools to tell their story and to adjust and adapt to each moment. This gives the leader confidence that the stories underneath the narrative, though told in a variety of voices, will be consistent. They don't have to do it all.

5. I do this because there is a power that has been used since the dawn of time to connect us, and that is the power of story. I know how to use this power and make it practical. When they can tell the right story in the right moment, they make a connection. When they make a connection, they build trust and increase their engagement and impact.

My brand story: I connect through the power of story.

As you go through these prompts for your brand, it's important to start with your audience. Many great tools exist to help you figure out your ideal customer, and any of them can help you do this. What helps me is thinking about why I love them. Once I know what it is about my ideal customer that makes me passionate about solving their problem, I can move to the next two steps: universal and specific. I move to the specific problem first, because that helps me find the universal theme.

When I think about my audience, I imagine what they're going through. I'm looking for trouble and find it in their daily activities. Once I look at their specific problem, it's easier to bubble up and think about what they really need and want. Look back at Maslow's pyramid if you need help finding their wants and needs. Once you know what they need, you can define how you help them meet that need.

Of course, we all want our work to serve everyone. Everyone should buy this book! This widget! Our services! They'll help everyone! True, they will. If you want to make an impact, however, you need to speak into the lives of those nearest to you. When you identify your target audience, you're looking into the eyes of the person you care about. The one you most want to serve.

Do I think this book can help everyone? Yes, I do! I think marketing executives and CEOs of Fortune 500 companies would benefit from this information. How do I get it to them? By zeroing in on the two or three people in front of me in the Italy pavilion at eleven thirty in the morning. By looking them in the eyes. Making them my friends. Saying, "Let's do something great together." When we look up, we may find there are ten, twenty, even two hundred people who've gathered to find out what we're doing that's so much fun and beneficial for those original three people.

The people I love are those who start with an idea and launch a business—authors, speakers, entrepreneurs, and non-profit leaders. I love you. I believe the work we do together would also benefit CEOs of gazillion-dollar companies. But just like on the streets at Epcot, when I performed a pre-show for five or ten people, only to look up and see that the joy we shared was so compelling, three hundred people flooded the street to join us, I believe the impact of what we share together here can radiate out. It's fine if it doesn't. It'll be our secret. They're welcome to join us.

Figure out who you're passionate about serving and get in close. Serve that ideal customer. As you solve their problem and share the stories of that success, word will spill out to others. Let the work do the work for you.

Once you know who you're talking to and what problem you can solve for them, you can edit your answers to the five questions and create one brand narrative. Build your own brand story and sentence. I got to my slimmed-down version by starting with my audience, stating their problem and my solution, and closing with the results the customer gets when they use it.

Gallery of Stories

When you have your brand story, you can curate a gallery of stories about the work your organization does. This is about the specifics—those examples filled with rich detail that paint the picture of your mission. And by gallery, I literally mean a gallery. Have five to seven stories at the ready that exemplify your theme.

When I was a trainer for actors at Walt Disney World, I encouraged performers to imagine they had a holster, but instead of a six-shooter at their hip, they had six comedy bits. These were stories or jokes they could toss into any situation to "Yes, And" the audience's offer and make the guest the star. When you have several stories at hand, you're not meeting every moment from a blank page.

You want several stories that serve different audiences. So, for example, if I were the communications director of a food bank that served several counties, I would use the story of the potato truck at the rest stop and all the volunteers who came with their pickups that night in order to win an audience that cares about reach and impact. That would be my base story. Then I'd follow one Ford Explorer filled with potatoes and tell the story of that volunteer—why they took that late-night call, why they came out, and what they want. That would work for an audience that wants to know about involvement. I'd also find out where that Ford Explorer went—what pantry it went to—and tell the story of a family who got a pound of those potatoes and made Nana's potato salad recipe with them. I'd share this story with people who want to know about the lives your organization changes. You could discover four or five stories from this one incident. Follow the stories and the people making those stories in your organization.

Make a list of the stories you use now on your website, in brochures, or in any speeches given by you or members of your team. Follow those stories to see if there are other characters in them whose stories could also be told. List out those potential stories. Then go back to your target audience and sketch out information about them. Start with the segment of your audience you currently connect with best. Then look at those with whom you want to develop a connection. Compare your list of stories with the two or three audiences you can reach, and see which stories will guide which audience to the best solution.

Needs and Wants

We've talked about the hero having a want and your audience having a need. This is so important that it bears saying again. It's the most important tool I bring to writing and speaking from my actor's toolbox.

While wants and needs go together, they're different. Wants connect with the "Universal so we can relate" portion of the Story Formula. Needs line up with "Specific so we care." I often say needs are immediate and visual, while wants are aspirational and visionary.

Think about some of our classic story heroes and the difference between their wants and needs. The story of Dorothy in *The Wizard of Oz* ends if she puts Toto on a leash. That's what she needed to do to keep him out of Miss Gulch's flowers. She doesn't want to do that, though, because she wants Toto to be free. She wants to be free too. Her highest want is consistent throughout the story, no matter what happens along the way. The circumstances dictate her needs—she needs to follow the yellow brick road, she needs to get out of the castle, she needs to find the wizard. But her want is dictated only by her heart—she wants to find life over the rainbow and the freedom that comes with it.

When actors first get a script, they dive into what's written, or what we call the "given circumstances." They look at the dialogue, the setting, the stage direction. On the next look, they read it with a different eye—one that asks "Why are these characters in this scene? What do they want?" The characters aren't there just because the playwright put them in that scene, although having written my fair share of scenes for corporate events, sometimes it really is just because the playwright needed a person to come in and announce, "There's a storm coming—take cover!" But as an actor, you can't play that.

If you enter a scene because you, the actor, are supposed to, there's no energy behind it. But if you enter because your character wants to save the town or needs to save himself and raises the stakes even higher by looking for his employer's niece, Dorothy, in the crowd, then you have a reason to be there, and it's a powerful reason. The audience won't know any of those things. They aren't going to hear that backstory. But they'll feel the importance of your character entering, scanning the crowd, and yelling, "Take cover—there's a storm coming!"

We don't do anything unless we have a deep want that leads to the need to do it. Really, we don't. I've needed jobs before and have taken many that served only the purpose of paying the bills. Those jobs didn't last long because the want—to be useful, to be fulfilled, to enjoy my own gifts and talents, and for someone else to enjoy my gifts and talents—is so strong, it's driven me to leave jobs I needed. I'm betting you've had a similar experience, where a situation was no longer tenable because your want for something was so strong.

Our wants and needs drive everything we do, as do the wants and needs of every character in every story. They also drive every audience member. The only reason they're listening to your story is because of their own wants and needs. It isn't their need to listen to your story. It's a want and need they have to be fulfilled in their own lives and work. Your job is to figure out what they want and need and then to give it to them in the form of a story, which is the best way for them to take in information.

Controlling Idea

The controlling idea is used in screenwriting to identify the theme of the story. In nonfiction writing, you craft a controlling idea and then list the ways you want to prove that idea true. Think of it as the topic sentence in a paragraph. You start with one thought, and it controls everything that follows it. If there's extraneous detail that doesn't support your controlling idea, out it goes. Find a place for it in another story, or tell two stories.

Every chapter of this book has a controlling idea of its own. The exercises, stories, and tools in each one prove the controlling idea to be true. The book as a whole has a controlling idea too, which is to discover the power of story. Each chapter in the book needs to prove that controlling idea. When writing the opening story for this chapter, I had to ask, "Does it prove the controlling idea that one universal brand story must drive every specific story?" If it didn't, out it went until I found the right story. The story of being the Fairy Godmother in the Utilidor was my third attempt. And now you know…the rest of the story.

Right Tools for the Job

When we moved into our new house, several things needed fixing. There were important things, like a broken kitchen counter, an air conditioner on the fritz, and a pool pump that needed to be replaced. And then there was another thing, which was the garage door. It squealed and crunched and creaked whenever it moved. We lived with the wrenching noise for over a year, attending to the other priorities. During that year, we gathered names and numbers of garage door specialists.

Then one Saturday, my husband got out a ladder and looked at each of the joints. All morning, the door screamed up and down as he examined each spot. Then he headed off to Lowe's. He came back with oil and WD-40, moved the cars out, and spent the rest of the day greasing each joint and scrubbing them with a wire brush. By the end of the day, the floor was full of rust and oil spots. He washed the garage floor and—voila!— smooth, quiet door. Now the neighbors don't even know when we're leaving.

It cost under fifteen dollars to fix the garage door, but we lived with the screeching noise for a year because other important things required our immediate attention. We were sure it would cost several hundred dollars to replace or fix the garage door. We just knew it would require a specialist. Once we turned our attention to it, however, the cost was minimal and the effects long lasting. What it took was the right tools and a few hours of dedicated attention.

This is what you need to do to improve your ability to share your story. With the right tools and a bit of attention, you'll be able to find exactly the right story for each moment. You'll master your nerves to speak in front of large groups or one-on-one with a potential client. You'll craft great social media posts for every outlet. Best of all, you'll be able to give these same tools to your team.

Once you develop a brand narrative and share the tools, you can trust that your staff will also tell the right story at the right moment. You can be confident they'll gather great stories for you to share on your website, in grant applications, and in interviews because they'll know how to make a connection. It'll be one less thing for you to think about. You have your tools and you know how to use them.

Relief. That's what I see when I lead workshops. People's shoulders come down from their ears, and they smile. If they started the day anxious and nervous, they end the day relieved. Sometimes they come nervous because public speaking isn't their thing. Sometimes they start on the defensive, thinking, "What do I need this for? I know my organization's story. After all, it's my passion that launched the thing. I know everything about my business." Once they start gaining tools to make their stories better and adaptable to any situation, they drop the defensiveness. When you're the one managing every detail of a business, it's a relief to find an easy system to handle an important part of the business.

When you use these tools, you can take any incident and turn it into a story. You can take an experience and make it into a "Once Upon a Time" story. You can write down what happened and quickly run through the "Five Ws" of Where, Who, When, What, and How to get the specifics, and then drill up to the Why and find the universal. For every e-newsletter and every proposal I write, I first populate a blank page with two words: *universal* and *specific*. I fill that out and then start on the e-newsletter below those words. I refer back as I go, making sure I've hit upon those points. Then I remove my notes before I press send.

Knowing you have the right story to tell in the right moment is all about the audience. I need to know who the audience is before I enter a room. What is it they have to offer? What need do they have that I might fulfill? When you're about to ask for a sale (if you're in business) or a donation (if you're a nonprofit), you must know how your ask solves the problem of the person in front of you.

When I know the wants or needs of the people in front of me, I get to be the Fairy Godmother. I offer them a pumpkin for a coach and get them where they want to go. In the story of Cinderella, the prince needs a bride and Cinderella needs to get out of the house. What he has to offer is a ball. Look at an ask in that same way—you, as the Fairy Godmother, are providing an opportunity and creating the right environment, whether it's a pumpkin coach, a mouse footman, or a glass slipper. You give them a timeline—by midnight, or all of this goes away.

Being the Fairy Godmother is better than being Cinderella. I know this for sure. I've been a character actress since I was twelve. I played the sweet, young thing once when I was four-teen, and it was a failure. I should have played the mother. I was always the mother, the aunt, or the best friend. Always the Fairy Godmother, never Cinderella.

Here's the great thing about being the character actor and not the ingenue. I get to keep playing this part in every season of my life. The ingenue, or hero, finally figures it out and overcomes whatever problem she had and moves on. She lives happily ever after, and that is the end of her story.

When you play the Fairy Godmother, you're always in the role of the mentor who gives people a path to their victory. It's been my privilege to actually be the Fairy Godmother—so take it from me. It may feel like you want to be Cinderella, but the Fairy Godmother is the way to go.

Cast a Wide Net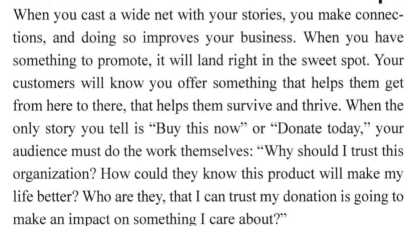

When you cast a wide net with your stories, you make connections, and doing so improves your business. When you have something to promote, it will land right in the sweet spot. Your customers will know you offer something that helps them get from here to there, that helps them survive and thrive. When the only story you tell is "Buy this now" or "Donate today," your audience must do the work themselves: "Why should I trust this organization? How could they know this product will make my life better? Who are they, that I can trust my donation is going to make an impact on something I care about?"

When you tell your story through everything you do, you build that connection with the audience right in front of you. Then you look up and find a larger network of people listening and invested in what you have to offer. The moral is, you can tell your story in a way that connects with your audience and develops a path for even more of them to connect with you.

Takeaways:

✓ Telling a story is harder than a formula. There's magic outside the formula, and that magic is you.

✓ You need to know and tell two stories: your brand story and the daily stories.

✓ Your brand story is the larger umbrella under which every daily story lives. It is not your origin story. It's the story of the problem you solve.

✓ When you see activities and behaviors that express your vision, you can start to see the story of your brand.

✓ To help discover your brand story, think about the passion you have for the people you serve and why you care about their problem.

✓ Once you know your brand story, you can create a gallery of daily stories to support it.

✓ If you want to make an impact, you need to speak into the lives of those nearest to you.

✓ Be the Fairy Godmother. It's better than being Cinderella.

Conclusion

Fire Circle

I t's your turn to experience the fire circle. Your turn to gather the energy of the people sitting around it and drive that energy through a story. You have more stories to tell than just one story. Your story is bigger than your origin story. You can connect with more people when you can find your deeper story and craft examples that tell that story in every situation.

You need to be able to tell your story. Most of the nonprofit leaders, entrepreneurs, writers, and speakers I work with are like you—people with a passion who had an idea. That idea launched an organization. You gathered a few loyal followers, and soon you were moving forward.

That forward movement led to a moment of growth, the opportunity for you to reach a wider audience. Then you were asked to give a speech. Pitch to a high-stakes client. You need to update your website. Maybe you've bolstered your solo venture with a team, and now they need to tell your story in an authentic way too—but still in your way. Maybe you need to relaunch after a global pandemic, economic meltdown, or other unplanned disaster (see murder hornets, recessions, hurricanes, locusts).

The bottom line is, it's time for you to reach a wider audience.

What really stands in your way, what really causes you to freeze at the sight of a blank page, is not nerves or fear that you're a good enough storyteller. Your biggest obstacle is this fear, prompted by these questions: "Will I be seen? Will I be heard? Will they get me?" That's what we really want to know. We're the Whos of Whoville, crying out, "We are here! We are here! We are here! We are here!" Without that perfectly timed "Yopp!" that breaks through the sound barrier, we're just a speck on a dandelion in an elephant's trunk.

To be seen and heard, you must be able to use the power of story. You must be able to tell stories in multiple formats for a variety of situations. You must train your team to tell your story in their own organic way while maintaining the integrity of the brand story.

But remember, it's not *just* your story. The essence of a story is one that connects. The story of your company, your passion, your product, or your idea is trying to connect with your audience. In a way, your story is about to become their story. Your audience is ready to get bigger—and to do that, they want and need to make your story their story.

Don't lose them by staying small. Paint a picture with words, and invite your audience to be the star of your show. Let their imagination paint the details, and watch them bond with you. Use the tools in this book to help you develop and deliver compelling stories. Refresh your story often by trying a different tool. Flip the script. Change up a specific detail. Find a deeper want.

Your story deserves it. And we want to hear you tell your story.

Acknowledgments

E very great story has a variety of characters who bring the world to life. My story is no different, and to the people who helped bring this story to life, thank you.

Gratitude goes to my friends who were my first readers for their notes—Randy, Rhonda, Louis, and Clare. And to the Morgan James Publishing team, who shared their wisdom, ideas, and designs.

The Victory Cup Initiative has been the very best incubator for this work, and I'm deeply grateful to the founder, Ashley Vann, for her support. It is a true privilege to do the deep work of story coaching with those leading the nonprofits in our community.

Speaking of deep work, my coach Elizabeth Dean gave me the tools to grow and flourish, and I wouldn't have gotten here without her. It's also a very good idea to ask a spiritual director if she'll be your editor. I'm so delighted that Christianne Squires said yes and for her insightful, detailed editing of this book.

I've had the great joy of doing story work over the years with my Disney family, the many arts organizations in Orlando, the Broadway community, and now my DTGO/MQDC family. Thank you for inviting me to help you tell your stories.

Thank you to my friends, especially the SAK Sisters—Diana, Morgan, Phran, Rhonda, and Stacy—and my walk-and-talk weekly, Sarah Lee Dobbs. Also to my brother and sister and my incredible parents, great storytellers all.

The best story is the love story I get to live out every day with my husband, Mohamed, and my talk-show-host son, Henry.

Additional Resources

There's more to help you tell your story.

At alicefairfax.com and tellyourstorybook.com, you can find PDF worksheets for exercises mentioned in this book, as well as additional resources. Just pop in your email address and download the worksheets for free.

While you're there, learn about Alice's online courses and upcoming live workshops. For in-depth interviews with storytelling experts, listen to Alice on the StoryMaven podcast wherever you get your podcasts.

About the Author

Alice Fairfax is senior vice president of ideation and experience design at MQDC, a destination development company headquartered in Bangkok, Thailand. She holds a certificate in creativity and innovation from the Walt Disney Company and Harvard Business School Publishing, as well as a BA in liberal arts from Rollins College. She is the author of *The Creative Life*.

An award-winning actor and writer, Fairfax was an improvisational storyteller at Walt Disney World for over twenty years, where she performed comedy on the streets of Epcot, told holiday stories around the world, coached singers at the *American Idol* Experience, and was "friends" with one iconic character (hint: she owns a magic wand and turns pumpkins into vehicles).

Alice leads Tell Your Story workshops and coaching sessions especially to help nonprofits and small businesses win the day with their stories. Alice lives with her family in Winter Garden, Florida, so close to the Magic Kingdom, they can hear the fireworks every night.

Endnotes

1   "Oprah Winfrey's Cecil B. DeMille Award Acceptance Speech—2018 Golden Globe Awards," YouTube video, 9:40, televised by NBC on January 7, 2018, posted by NBC, December 30, 2019, https://www.youtube.com/watch?v=TTyiq-JpM-0.

2   Stephen Halliwell, The Poetics of Aristotle: Translation and Commentary (Chapel Hill: University of North Caroline Press, 1987), 34.

3   Donald Miller and Mike McHargue, "Why People Buy: The Powerful Science of Selling—Interview with 'Science Mike' McHargue," no date, in Building a StoryBrand, produced by Tim Schurrer, podcast, 29:13, https://buildingastorybrand.com/episode-2/; Donald Miller and

Mike McHargue, "Mike McHargue—The Science of Why Your Brain Needs a Villain," no date, in Business Made Simple, podcast, 40:08, https://podcasts.apple.com/us/podcast/mike-mchargue-the-science-of-why-your-brand-needs-a-villain/id1092751338?i=1000427616201.

4   David Eagleman, as quoted in Dennis Pierce, "What Neuroscience Teaches Us about Fostering Creativity," THE Journal, June 25, 2018, https://thejournal.com/articles/2018/06/25/what-neuroscience-teaches-us-about-fostering-creativity.aspx.

5   Eric Almquist, John Senior, and Nicolas Bloch, "The Elements of Value," Harvard Business Review, September 2016, https://hbr.org/2016/09/the-elements-of-value.

6   Malcolm Gladwell, The Tipping Point: How Little Things Can Make a Big Difference (Boston: Back Bay, 2002), 24–25.

7   Stephen King (@StephenKing), Twitter, July 30, 2019, 11:59 a.m., https://twitter.com/StephenKing/status/1156232944853405697?s=20.

8   David Byrne and Amy Schumer, April 2020, in Amy Schumer Presents: 3 Girls, 1 Keith, https://open.spotify.com/episode/3oHiChsIjNTDe0X8QNDshy?si=rvTi69haR5OtfMJU2H-fow.

9   Emma Coats, as quoted in Cyriaque Lamar, "The Twenty-Two Rules of Storytelling, According to Pixar," Gizmodo, June 8, 2012, https://io9.gizmodo.com/the-22-rules-of-storytelling-according-to-pixar-5916970.

10 Chris Anderson, TED Talks: The Official TED Guide to Public Speaking (Mariner Books: New York, 2017), 66–67.

11 William Shakespeare, prologue to Henry V, lines 1–4, as quoted in Folger Shakespeare Library, https://www.folger. edu/explore/shakespeares-works/henry-v/read/PRO/.

12 Billy Collins, "Everyday Moments, Caught in Time," TED video filmed as part of TED2012, 14:57, https://www.ted. com/talks/billy_collins_everyday_moments_caught_in_ time?language=en.

13 Anne Lamott, "Twelve Truths I Learned from Life and Writing," TED video filmed as part of TED2017, 15:45, https://www.ted.com/talks/anne_lamott_12_truths_i_ learned_from_life_and_writing.

A free ebook edition is available with the purchase of this book.

To claim your free ebook edition:

1. Visit MorganJamesBOGO.com
2. Sign your name CLEARLY in the space
3. Complete the form and submit a photo of the entire copyright page
4. You or your friend can download the ebook to your preferred device

Morgan James
BOGO™

A **FREE** ebook edition is available for you or a friend with the purchase of this print book.

CLEARLY SIGN YOUR NAME ABOVE

Instructions to claim your free ebook edition:
1. Visit MorganJamesBOGO.com
2. Sign your name CLEARLY in the space above
3. Complete the form and submit a photo of this entire page
4. You or your friend can download the ebook to your preferred device

Print & Digital Together Forever.

Snap a photo

Free ebook

Read anywhere

Printed in the USA
CPSIA information can be obtained
at www.ICGtesting.com
JSHW021407201123
52414JS00003B/35